Acclaim for Springs Toledo's
SMOKESTACK LIGHTNING

"[A] fascinating biography of a boxer who was avoided by Jack Dempsey and managed to beat almost every major heavyweight and light-heavy back in the good old days, despite the fact that he was only a middleweight! Springs Toledo brings 1919 to life in rich and colourful prose. An absolute must for any boxing fan and a compelling portrait of a man…"
—GRAHAM MINETT, author of *Anything for Her*

"Absorbing and richly detailed. Toledo offers enough evidence and detail to cause the reader to shake his head in disbelief at what no normal human being would seem capable of doing."
—MIKE SILVER, author of *Stars in the Ring*

"Like John L. Sullivan, Greb felt like he could 'Lick any sonofabitch in the world' and let everyone know it. But unlike John L., Greb actually set out to do so. His ferocious confidence leaps off the pages."
—DOUGLAS CAVANAUGH, boxing historian

"I never met Harry Greb, never saw him fight, but in *Smokestack Lightning* it's as if I did. Springs Toledo, with his intimate voice and vibrant prose, smashes through that seemingly impenetrable wall of time."
—ADAM BERLIN, author of *The Standing Eight*

ALSO BY SPRINGS TOLEDO

The Gods of War
In the Cheap Seats
Murderers' Row

SMOKESTACK
LIGHTNING

Mildred Reilly, circa 1918.

SMOKESTACK LIGHTNING

Harry Greb, 1919

SPRINGS TOLEDO

Cover photograph: "Pittsburgh by Night" circa 1907
Cover design by Springs Toledo
Book design by Springs Toledo

For the Tree of Life Synagogue, which has
become a living tribute to the strength,
resilience, and beauty of the Jewish people.

Epiphany Church, Pittsburgh, P.A. Author's photograph.

I. This Side of Paradise

He was late.

The ceremony, a Solemn High Mass at Greb's insistence, was set for 9:00 a.m. on January 30, 1919. Greb's manager, James "Red" Mason, had somehow convinced the couple to disregard a folk rhyme popular at the time and push the date up from Monday *(married on Monday, married for health)* to Thursday *(married on Thursday, married for losses)*. Pittsburgh itself was invited. Many of the thousand plus who attended were milling outside the church at 9:15, checking pocket watches and craning their necks on Washington Place. It was nearly 9:30 when taxis rumbled up and screeched to a stop.

A door clacked open as the crowd filed into the church and when the leg of the bride-to-be swung out to the running board, a few at the back sneaked a peek. Next came an arm and a gloveless hand as eighteen-year-old Mildred Kathleen Reilly was assisted out and onto the street, a wide-brimmed hat pulled low in the fashion of the day. She wore a dark blue travelling suit and lipstick like Clara Bow—still something of a scandal as the Jazz Age dawned.

Pittsburgh Press, 2/6/1919.

On her finger was a diamond. A karat and a half, set on a platinum band. It sparkled like some low-hanging star plucked from the sky.

Nearby was her mother. She knew that Mildred would have done exactly that, if she could, reach up through the smoke and the sprawl of Pittsburgh and pluck a star if it caught her eye. She'd tweak the thumb of the angel who held it too. Mrs. Reilly knew better than anyone that her eldest daughter was a willful girl.

Did she wonder at her that morning? She may have been in a swoon of relief. After all, only three years had passed since Mildred disappeared from home, missed her fifteenth birthday, and scared her half to death. It was a Tuesday in August when she told her mother that she was off to find work at a varnish company. It was a likely story. Her birthday was Wednesday and on Thursday "Police Seek Missing Girl" appeared in the *Daily Post*.

Nine days later, Mildred appeared in an alderman's office filing a suit to recover salary owed for her appearance in a film promoting the city's "Be-Brite" clean-up campaign. When asked her name and address, she was truthful. When asked her age, she was not. "Twenty," she said.

Mildred dreamed of being an actress. She appeared in amateur shows at the Nixon Theater on Sixth Avenue and likely a few others downtown before Mrs. Reilly found out and put her foot down. *No daughter of mine!* It echoes faintly down through the decades. The pandemonium a willful girl can bring to the home does too: the screaming and slamming doors, the sobbing in the bedroom, younger siblings wide-eyed and silent; the Irish mother, worn and haggard at thirty-seven, but with eyes afire and a brogue turned stern. There was no Mr. Reilly to lean on, to turn to when things got bad. Mildred was seven when he died from a perforation of the bowel in Indiana where he found a job as a railroad brakeman. He was always looking for a way up. Mildred was looking for a way out.

In December 1915, the *Pittsburgh Sun* ran an article written by that era's Miley Cyrus that began with the headline "Anita Stewart Tells Girls How to Achieve Success and Happiness." Framed as a "heart-to-heart talk to girls," it began by undermining mothers: "How can the mother who knows only the problems of her own home be a guide to her daughter who is living the life of a stage actress?"

The day the article appeared on newsstands, Mildred went to a pharmacy and bought a bottle of blue triloids—poison. At midnight, she took the cork out and crushed and scattered four tablets on the floor by her bed. Then she rubbed one on those Clara Bow lips to make them blister.

"Mother! Mother!" she screamed. "I have taken poison!"

An aunt and uncle living on nearby Meyran Avenue got involved and the police were called. As the officers administered first aid, they told her she was being taken to the hospital, and Mildred, realizing she'd gone too far this time, blurted out that the whole thing was just a stunt. No one believed her.

At the Homeopathic Hospital, doctors stuck hypodermic needles into her arm—that was "fierce," she told a reporter—and kept her under close watch for symptoms that never appeared.

Her stunt worked. By January 1917, she was working at the Victoria, a new burlesque house at 956 Liberty Avenue, around the corner from the Nixon. She had a specialty act that could have been a bawdy song, a racy (though not nude) dance, or a comedy sketch. It was evidently well received because by March she had a supporting role in a burletta called "Hotel Uproar" that featured a night clerk causing "indescribable confusion" among guests and "proved a scream from beginning to end."

Was Mrs. Reilly in the audience? Almost certainly not. But someone else almost certainly was.

Harry Greb emerged from the idling taxi wearing a fur-collared coat over a fashionable suit, his dark hair slicked back and the sides of his head shaved clean. A reporter made a note about his "natty appearance in the role of groom."

He was a nervous wreck.

Born June 6, 1894 to a stone mason of severe character from Germany and a mother with roots in

Prussia and Bavaria, Greb grew up in a household where schnitzel and sauerkraut were staples, where hard work and good manners were expected and *Deutsch* was spoken.

He was baptized "Eduard Henry" on June 10 at St. Joseph's, a German-Catholic parish in the Bloomfield neighborhood of Pittsburgh where he attended school and received the sacraments. Only later did he adopt the name "Harry" after a baby brother who died in the crib. Six children were born to Pius and Anna, of whom four survived into adulthood. Greb was the eldest with three sisters behind him.

He was awkward, had a lazy eye, and was often the butt of jokes. "A quiet boy," his father said. "The other boys teased him but he wouldn't fight back." Regis Toomey, who lived a few doors down on North Millvale Street, remembered them mimicking his mother when she called him home. He had nicknames that sound like slights. "Bunny" is a term of endearment for someone a little lost or confused. He was also called "Moon Face," though "Icky" or "Ick" stuck to him for years. "When very small," Ida, the sister closest to him tells us, "he used to say 'icky' for chickens" and was himself "as fat as a butterball up to the time he was 10 years old."

He received First Communion on June 23, 1907 at the unusually late age of thirteen. The child's confessor, working with the parents, can defer the Blessed Sacrament to adolescence for reasons including spiritual immaturity, especial devotion, or a cultural practice carried over from Europe (and which earned the Pope's censure in 1910). On a Sunday afternoon in May 1908, not two months after an older sister died of endocarditis at fifteen, Greb was among one hundred seventy-five confirmed by the bishop at St. Joseph's. The name he chose for the sacrament is a clue that he was trying to redefine himself and his place in the world—"Alphons" has Germanic roots and means *ready for a fight.*

Snapshots from these transformative years skitter across the historical record. Greb, standing atop a stool in the basement and proclaiming himself not only a winner, but "champion of the world!" Greb tied to a wagon wheel by five bullies, then freeing himself and flying into "a wild rage." A neighbor's mother thwacking him with an umbrella while he all but murdered a larger boy who had taken something from him. The adolescent battles for independence against his father's old-world expectations.

Ill-equipped to sit still and learn by rote—he was a walking checklist for ADHD—he quit school. He appears in the 1909 city directory as a "gas fitter" and was seen hanging around storefronts on Penn Avenue—"loafing," Pius might have sniffed, or looking for trouble. The 1910 census indicates that he was fifteen the last time he showed up in a classroom, though it is believed he didn't advance past the sixth grade. He bounced from one low-level job to another: an errand boy at a downtown firm, stints at Lepper and Bauer's Hardware Store on Butler Street and Graff Brothers, a roofing and sheet metal company on Penn Ave. At sixteen, he was an electrician's apprentice at Westinghouse Electric. He ran there every morning to strengthen his legs.

On Saturday nights, he'd take a trolley downtown to the fights at Old City Hall and sat mesmerized in the dark. Boxing became an obsession, though he showed no promise. He was routinely licked in boyhood scraps and his friends snickered at his dream; his father dead-set against it. His earliest instructor, at least the earliest mentioned by name, was Rabbit Smoots, an ex-pug who lived nearby and taught him that the sweet science ain't so sweet with regular beatings in his kitchen.

But it was the Church Militant that ensured the teenager's transformation. Across the street from Epiphany, at 110 Washington Place, was the Lyceum. It had a boxing ring. In 1903, Reverend Lawrence A. O'Connell, the founding pastor of Epiphany who was as much a social worker as a priest, borrowed $50,000 to purchase a two-story building to give Pittsburgh's young men something to do. It did more than that for Icky Greb. It gave him something to hold onto. "He had no friends, no place to train," said Father James Cox, who ran the Lyceum, "and [he] begged me to be permitted to join."

After an amateur career lasting less than a month, he fought in a smoker and was paid $12. "There was no stopping him," admitted his father, who at some point drove him out of the family home at 138 North Millvale—*no son of mine!* an echo in his ear.

By the fall of 1915, Greb was renting rooms at 114 North Millvale. He stayed close. Twenty-one and already forty-four fights into a professional boxing career, his voice can be heard in local newspapers. It is the voice of a brash and reckless young man.

A little past two on a Sunday in September, a group of brash and reckless young men confronted one Clarence Jackson at the corner of Penn and Mathilda, a block up from North Millvale. They objected to what they said was Jackson's "unseemly conduct." Greb was there and said he and a friend "remonstrated with Jackson for the latter's actions before girls," which implies it was something more than an interracial conversation that caught their attention. A crowd formed and things got rough, especially for Jackson, who offered to fight any one of them. Greb stepped forward. Predictably, Jackson took a beating and then surprised everyone by pulling a gun and firing, narrowly missing Greb and injuring his friend with a bullet in the jaw. Early reports said that Greb rushed him, "and would yah believe it, I brushed those bullets away from me before they got started," he laughed. "I'm getting fast with my hands."

Jackson took off running and Greb chased him, followed by a crowd of men and boys. Jackson barricaded himself in a house by Allegheny Cemetery and fired several more shots from a second story window before police arrived.

Charged with felonious assault and battery, Jackson told the court a different story than Greb's. He said he was attacked for no reason by a mob and had to shoot to save his skin. In November, he was sentenced to one year in the Allegheny County workhouse.

Jackson was no angel. An individual sharing his name was accused of breaking into the supply room of the Pennsylvania Railroad and taking $1500 worth of copper wire in 1907. The same name appears in a December 1916 edition of the *Pittsburgh Press* as having been found guilty of slashing someone with a razor during what looks like a robbery.

As for Greb, he dashed from one thing to another. That evening he signed a contract to face a hard-punching coal miner named George Chip. His manager conceded much to make the fight, but Greb didn't mind. He was willing to take on guys who outweighed him by twenty pounds and didn't believe anyone outgunned him even if they had a gun and he didn't. And this was a statement fight—Chip was the former middleweight champion of the world. It was also a no-decision bout, an inaptly named "exhibition" as Pennsylvania would not officially legalize boxing until 1923. Greb didn't care; barring a knockout, newspaper writers were proxy judges and declared the winners in the morning edition.

Two weeks before the contest, Greb was antagonizing Chip. "You big stiff!" he said. "You fresh kid!" came the retort, which everyone agreed was true. The six-round fight was a draw. They hadn't left the ring yet when Greb called Chip "an unprintable name" and they were at it again.

It was sometime in 1917 when he met Mildred Reilly, probably at the Victoria. Given his devil-may-care disposition and her ambitions, it was anything but a traditional courtship. F. Scott Fitzgerald might have used them as models for *The Beautiful and the Damned*— fun-loving with a taste for finer things, defiant, prone to use slang and coarse language—life for them was a whirligig, a windmill. Liberty Avenue was three miles from Greb's front door. He could run there inside of twenty minutes or she could come to him, and probably did.

She was the love of his life. Had World War I not disrupted their plans, they would have been married a year earlier. Greb registered for the war effort, placed in class 1-A of the draft in March 1918, and enrolled in the U.S. Naval Reserves in May. He was part of the recruiting effort in Manhattan until October, when he requested a transfer to the U.S.S. *Sierra* ("I desire sea duty" was the reason given). In early December, he was in London competing in the King's Tournament at Albert Hall. Before it began, he reportedly got into an argument and ended up fighting four Australians at once, going about even until he snatched a billy club off a bobby and chased them off. The next day he was hit by a car and woke up in a hospital. Not long after that he slipped, cracked his head on the tile floor of a Turkish bath, and ended up with several stitches. He tore off his bandages and competed anyway—and was eliminated early on a bum decision.

On December 17, 1918 his ship docked in New York and he caught a train home to Pittsburgh. The *Daily Post* caught up to him at the Southside Market House, just across the Tenth Street Bridge in Bedford Square, on Christmas. "I wouldn't trade the lower end of Fifth Avenue for all of London," he said.

Pittsburgh, early 20th century.

London-born novelist Anthony Trollope doubted anyone could see six feet in front of them at the lower end of Fifth Avenue. A stop in Pittsburgh—"the blackest place I ever saw," he wrote—compelled him to take a bath, and when he stepped out of the tub and onto the carpet, his foot left a print in the soot. Trollope was writing in 1862. Not much had changed by 1919. A party of literary travelers entering the city that year saw monstrous furnaces belching smoke, "obliterating the city and even the sky and sun." In the evening, they stood on a bridge looking at the steel mills lining the river. The atmosphere was "filled with sparks, jets of flame bursting through the smoke." Hell with the lid off.

On New Year's Day in 1919, Greb presented Mildred with that low-hanging star he'd plucked from the sky. It filled her eyes. She told the *Gazette Times'* Harry Keck that she "had everything planned for her husband"; that her Harry would become a king by the summer of 1920—at the latest. "I know he will win the championship, and I'll bet he'll land it under my management." She also planned to keep Greb in the middleweight division—like a normal human being with natural instincts of self-preservation—and leave those heavyweights and light heavyweights alone. That intention failed. Marriage steadied but did not quite civilize Greb, who went on to build his legend around what he did to heavyweights and light heavyweights, around a slogan he'd repeat again and again: *anybody, anyplace, anytime.*

Even so, he was happier than he'd ever been. Mildred filled his eyes. "I am confident that I can clean up the whole world now," he said.

January 1919 was a whirlwind of wedding planning, shopping sprees, house furnishing, and boxing matches. Between Tuesday the 14th and Monday the 27th, he fought four times in four cities and was just warming up. Every rival within reach of the railroads was put on notice—Greb was coming.

Rattling tracks and bellowing smokestacks, sparks flying, were his heralds.

Union Station today. Author's photograph.

II. I'd Go a Long, Long Way for You

Like a jet of flame bursting through the smoke of Pittsburgh, Harry Greb sets out to fight "them all, one after the other."

again. The door clanged shut. I jerked it and startled the concierge, who walked over and stuck his head out.

"Are you a resident?"

"Nah," I said. "I'm doin' research on a bygone era."

"There's no public access here. You got to be a resident," he eyed me curiously.

"You're from Boston aren't you." He wasn't asking.

"How'd yah know?" I had no need to ask.

He laughed and let me in.

"I can't kick it," I said.

"Why try?"

Larry was his name. A sixty-something African American whose army days were spent alongside an Irish American from Dorchester, he let me in because my accent brought him back to the 1970s.

"—the 1970s?" I said. "Man, I'm in 1919."

He walked me to the Grand Hall, what used to be the Union Station concourse—eleven thousand square feet of marble with vaulted ceilings, terra-cotta archways, a skylight streaming sunlight. "It's used for big events," he said. "You should see this space decked out for weddings. Like royalty." There's an antique clock at the center and a few restored railroad benches along the periphery. Relics. I saw Harry and Mildred hurrying by that clock and those benches, hand-in-hand, to catch the train.

Cleveland was no place for a honeymoon. It still isn't. The Grebs were putting that off—there was business to attend to and it was worth a grand to them, plus train tickets.

Outside the Cleveland station, newsboys hawked *The Plain Dealer*. The thirty-sixth state had recently ratified the Eighteenth Amendment, which would prohibit "the manufacture, sale, or transportation of intoxicating liquors" though the news was as ignored as the law itself would be. It appeared on page eight like an afterthought, lost between ads for an electric ice machine and a yearbook for a meat-packing company.

The Grebs headed to a friend's house to spend the night.

At 3:40 Friday, already forty minutes late to the weigh-in for that evening's fight with Tommy Robson, Greb was feasting in the Cleveland Athletic Club's dining room as if it were a second reception. There was an obligatory argument between managers before Greb, stuffed and fully clothed, stepped on the scale. Too heavy and likely hungover, he went ten rounds. At the end of it, still feeling amorous for obvious reasons, he planted two kisses on Robson's forehead and left the ring without a scratch.

Robson was amazed at what he couldn't do:

> I had seen him fight three times before and thought it would be easy for a man of my hitting powers to straight[en] him up when he came leaping in and then hand him the old kayo. That's where I fooled myself. He came jumping at me and I would set guard against his right when from somewhere his left would flash and I would take it twice without giving him even a jab. The next time I would be prepared for his left and he would bring a wild, awkward right swing from somewhere behind him and chop me with it. He did not hurt me but never before did anyone hit me so often and get away without any damage to speak of.
>
> Now the question is, 'How does he do it?' How can any man of his weight dance and leap and keep on top of you the way he does without becoming exhausted? And he can go twenty rounds the same way. He is the biggest freak in the ring, and I know the only way I will ever be able to beat him is to land a haymaker and with him sprawling all over me I don't see how I can do it.

Robson wasn't alone in his attempt to explain the inexplicable. Sports writers depleted ink wells trying to deconstruct his style—"the Pittsburgh pandemonium," they'd say. "Demon driver." "The personification of speed itself." And more assets were coming to light. "There doesn't seem to be any connection between Greb's jaw and his nerve centre," said the *Buffalo Commercial*. He is "endowed with the strength of a bull and the belief that he can't be hurt."

But he did a lot of hurting. Reports abound of opponents spitting blood, nursing a broken rib or a broken nose, groping their way back to the corner with eyes swollen shut. Greb "came into the ring," said a contemporary, "with everything but a hand grenade and a machine gun."

When he invaded one city, fans would write letters to newspapers in the next. *Don't miss him*, they'd say. "Although you may not like his strange style at first, you can't help but fall in love with it later on, just on account of his speed and ability to hit from any angle, and so after that his opponent is bewildered and before he can fathom his style," said one, he's "a licked man."

On Saturday February 1, Harry and Mildred disembarked at Union Station and settled into a newly furnished home he'd purchased outright at 257 Gross Street.

On Monday, February 3, he fought at the Southside Market House, barely broke a sweat, and was razzed for defeating a no-hoper. His response? On the 10th he was in Syracuse looking up at six-foot Bill Brennan, one of the best heavyweights in the world.

Greb's fun began in the elegant Onondaga Hotel. "I'm standing in the lobby, you know, right up near the desk," he said. "In comes a bunch of sports from some little town nearby. They're friends of Brennan's. They don't know me from Adam."

They were hoping for a live one, preferably "any friends of this fellow Harry Greb." One of them flashes a bankroll and said they want to lay down a bet that Brennan knocks Greb out.

"You look like a sport," he said to Greb.

"I'm sure he's kidding me," Greb figured, before realizing none of them had any idea who he was. "—How much?"

"Oh, a couple of hundred."

"Wanna bet $500?"

"The bet is on—," Greb said.

The pair strolled to a cigar stand nearby. "I'm just reaching for a cigar, a nice big expensive smoke, when up comes one of the bellboys. 'Mr. Greb, you're wanted on the telephone.' The small town sport looks at me. He stopped smiling."

They had left the scene by the time Greb came out of the booth. He next saw them at ringside Monday night. "You should have heard them babies yell for Brennan to knock me crazy," he laughed. "They yelled round after round. They got their $500 back in free yells."

It was a furious fight, though there was no doubt whose fight it was. In the last round, Brennan had nothing left. Greb grabbed him in a clinch and wheeled him around so he could look over a shoulder at the sap who bet against him.

"How do you feel now?"

"I'm suffering internally," came the response. "And the rest of the boys are close to death!"

The *Syracuse Herald* and the *Post-Standard* agreed that Greb didn't lose one of the ten rounds.

At 5:30 Wednesday afternoon, he hopped on the Empire State Express at Syracuse and hopped off at Buffalo. While he and Red Mason lugged their baggage across the platform to board the Pittsburgh train, reporters from both the *Courier* and the *Enquirer* remarked that he didn't have a mark on him. "Easy bout, dead easy, one of the softest I've had in a long time," Greb told them. "Just like picking cherries."

With a grand in his pocket and a big win behind him, Greb cut a dandyish figure. He carried a gold-topped cane and wore cloth-topped shoes, a blue serge suit (popular in 1919), a fur coat, and a pearl gray derby. When someone noted the diamond in his necktie looked like the bottom of a beer bottle, he told them he bought it off a bookie in London who'd gone broke at the races.

Brennan, he said, was a prelim for Battling Levinsky. "I've got an account to settle with that young man," he said. "We boxed once in Pittsburgh... In the first round, Levinsky clips me over the eye. Bing! I get a slit. Couldn't do my best after that. But he didn't sneak the decision. Not over me."

Levinsky's New York-based manager "Dumb" Dan Morgan had written a letter to the editor of the *Gazette Times*. "As for fighting and boxing ability, the Battler makes Greb look like a cart horse," that's right, he said, "a cart horse"; "the Merry–go-round kid"; "the Pittsburgh circus boy." And he added injury to insult when he sent out a phony wire that said Levinsky won the decision. "Greb never got over that, and has nursed his revenge," Mason said. "I'll trim Levinsky right this time," added Greb. "Wait and see."

But there was a problem. Greb was sparring on Sunday at the Berger building gym on Fourth Street and a cut opened over his left eye. Three stitches closed it. The fight was Monday. He wouldn't hear talk of a postponement, lugged his baggage to Union Station, and probably slept his way north on the night train.

"They fought with the speed of bantams," said the *Buffalo Commercial*. "The boxing was so fast the rounds faded like mist in the sun." Greb, true to form, was tearing in behind a fusillade; landing punches with his feet in mid-air and so busy he rarely bothered to set himself. Ringsiders watched him between rounds; he couldn't sit still on the stool.

Levinsky had a ten-pound weight advantage and several inches in height over Greb, but his direct shots to the jaw didn't do a thing. He didn't even disturb the stitches. "Twice Bat measured Greb perfectly and as he leaped in, jabbed with a left and whipped the right to the same mark, but Greb only smiled, crouched, leaped, and tried from another angle . . .Greb was forever coming," said the *Courier*. "There was no stopping Greb," said the *Commercial*. "How does he do it?" How is anyone's guess, though no small part of why was Mildred, sitting pretty—and pretty loudly—at ringside.

Levinsky lost big. He was downcast when he boarded the Empire State Express back home. "Maybe there'll be another day," he said.

Greb had fought on three consecutive Mondays and had a ten-day break before his next and last bout in February. "What in the world will poor Harry Greb do with himself the next week or so?" quipped the *Pittsburgh Daily Post.* "He'll probably have to go out in the streets and lick a coupla cops or something to keep feeling right."

Too restless to stay home, Greb was in New York City training at Grupp's Gym the next week and on Friday, February 28, he's at the Coliseum in Toledo fighting Chuck Wiggins in a sold-out show. Wiggins would "do anything," it was said, "but pull a knife on you in there." Greb hit Wiggins about ten thousand times.

On March 1, Greb was transferred to inactive duty in Pittsburgh and two days after that he's at the Elk's Auditorium in Detroit treating a still-damaged Wiggins like the "receiver-general."

Wiggins never got over those first two fights with Greb. Later in life, when all he had was a bottle of whiskey and muddled memories, he was often asked who his toughest opponent was. "I pick Greb!" he'd shout. "The worst beating of my career was given to me by that Dutchman Greb. He made me say 'Uncle' twice in three days."

On March 6, Greb gave Hall of Famer Leo Houck "the worst beating of his fighting career" in Houck's own hometown of Lancaster, Pennsylvania.

On March 17, Mildred watched him blitz Brennan again two miles from home at Duquesne Gardens.

He was back at it on the 25th and on the 31st defeated his third Hall of Famer that year in Billy Miske.

Greb was on track to eclipse the laurels he earned in 1917 for thirty-seven engagements. "He is never satisfied unless he has a half dozen or so mills booked ahead," said an observer. "HARRY GREB," said another, "FIGHTS ABOUT EVERY NIGHT and then walks around ALL DAY looking for TROUBLE." The furious pace he set in the ring was one thing; the madness of going once and sometimes two or three times a week quite another. Most fighters slept in hotels. Greb was getting his shut-eye on red-eyes or on a bench between trains. Mason once left him sleeping in the checkroom umbrella rack at Union Station.

On April 2, he was in Butler, Pennsylvania where he knocked out a heavyweight with a left uppercut to the jaw.

On April 7, he's up in Syracuse speeding all over Young Fisher.

Courtesy of Dan Robie.

On April 8, he turns up at the Iroquois Brewing Company in Buffalo laughing at the local sports who bet that George "One Round" Davis, a six-foot puncher, would knock him out. "Birds like Davis can't hit me with a buggy whip. I'm like Bob Fitzsimmons, who once said, 'the bigger they are the harder they fall.' Take a big fellow like Davis, slow moving, and I can have lots of fun banging away at him."

—And bang away he did. Mildred was ringside while Davis was forced backwards by "the leaping, bounding, elusive Greb, who kept both of his long arms going like flails."

On April 25, Greb was in Erie, Pennsylvania where Houck proved he still couldn't do a thing with him and on April 28 he's in Canton, Ohio where Levinsky could do no better.

In May, he took the night train to Boston to break Clay Turner's ribs, returned to Pittsburgh and "slam-banged" heavyweight Willie Meehan "literally to all parts of the ring," took another night train to Buffalo where he cut up the eyes of Bartley Madden, and skipped over to Syracuse where Tommy Robson gave up trying to hit him and covered up with both hands.

On June 10, with three fights lined up, he left Pittsburgh for the Atlantic City shore. On the 16th he was in Philadelphia where he went running to Mildred in the stands after the referee rescued Joe Borrell from "annihilation." That was Monday. On Wednesday, Greb was in Erie tearing up a heavyweight and on Friday he's in Wheeling, West Virginia tearing up another.

It was an astonishing pace. Harry Keck couldn't decide whether it was inhuman or superhuman.

Next in line was a legendary figure determined to end Greb's mad rush into boxing history. On June 21, Greb was on the morning train from Wheeling to Pittsburgh where he would face Mike Gibbons, the St. Paul Phantom himself. The sky blackened in his wake.

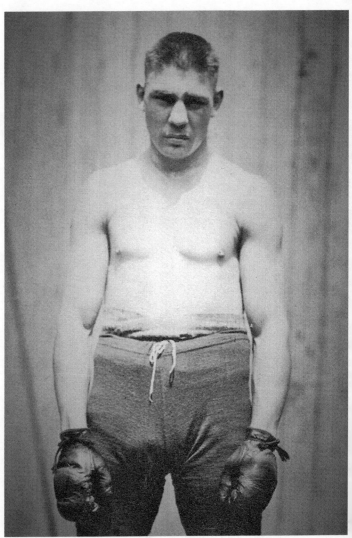

Photographer Frank Bingaman. Courtesy of Carnegie Library, Pittsburgh.

III. The Uncanny

It ain't business. It's personal.

R oy McHugh was a sports editor and columnist-at-large for the *Pittsburgh Press* until he retired in 1983. He's a hundred and three now; still living in the Smoky City with a treasure trove of memories. He told me he shook one of the dukes of the St. Paul Phantom himself in 1924, only five years after those dukes were flying at the head of Harry Greb.

McHugh spent his childhood in Cedar Rapids, Iowa. He was nine and in his pediatrician's waiting room when he picked up a copy of the *Boxing Blade* "and got hooked." His pediatrician was a friend of Mike Gibbons, who had a gym in St. Paul and was managing fighters at the time. When the once-great middleweight came to town, the good doctor introduced McHugh and his brother to him. A week

later a set of boxing gloves arrived at the boys' address.
A note was attached:

Put on these gloves and do your stuff,
Prepare for the days when roads are rough;
You'll get a little groggy, but just give bad luck an uppercut.

Greb-Gibbons II was scheduled for June 23, 1919.
Ringside seats sold for $10, $7.50 and $5. Grandstand
seats were $3 and $2 plus war tax. Requests for
reserved seats were coming in from towns and cities
across Ohio, Indiana, and West Virginia, particularly
those Greb had invaded. A contingent hanging around
the training camps of heavyweight champion Jess
Willard and challenger Jack Dempsey arrived in from
Toledo.

Seven thousand streamed into Forbes Field to see
what a master boxer could do against an avowed
anarchist the second time around. Gibbons had gotten
the better of him back in 1917 and figured he'd do it
again. Greb, favored to win and with bravado on
display, knew Gibbons was the goods. George A.
Barton, sports editor of the *Minneapolis Tribune* did too.
"A toss of the head, a slight twist of the body, and an
intended kayo punch will finish in a foolish wave to the
fans in the gallery," he said. Gibbons spent a novitiate

sparring with luminaries like Joe Gans and knew all the tricks that leave a "frustrated battler steaming about in fury."

That was exactly Greb's plan—steaming about in fury.

Jim Jab liked Mike. "Fistic class puzzles many mortals," he wrote in the first line of the next morning's *Pittsburgh Press*. "They fail to understand its fine points, its timing, feinting, and foiling. Among the hundreds of Pittsburgh fans…scores belonged to this clan." In his estimation, which was a lonely one, anarchy won no more than two of the ten rounds. The *Daily Post* and the AP gave Greb six to Gibbons' three with one even. The *Gazette Times* had Greb up six to two with two even.

Greb, avenged, took home $5,514.50 and continued on with the big get-even. In July, he caught up with Joe Chip in Youngstown, Ohio. Chip was and remains the only fighter to ever lay him out for the count. "It was funny how it all happened," said Greb about the 1913 match. "Everything was going along smoothly until Chip started a long swing… instead of ducking the swing, I ran flush into it." For days afterward, Greb said there were "sweetly caroling birds" in his head.

But he was a novice then. This time, he won all but one round. He toyed with Chip and laughed when his friends tried to spur him on. Hissed by the crowd and warned by the referee for using his head in close and for hitting in the clinches, he dropped his defense to let Chip do what he could in the last round. It wasn't much. Chip, under siege in the final seconds, was forced into a corner and turned his back.

Avenged again, Greb headed home and cooled his jets for a week. Mildred accompanied him to Conneaut Lake in the northern part of Pennsylvania. "Great guns!" blared a headline. "Greb Loafs for a While!" To Greb it was "a summer's rest." A friend wondered at that.

"Rest? Why you haven't rested at all!"

"Any time I'm not fighting three times a week," said Greb, "it's a vacation for me."

Columnists tended to present Greb as a clean-living young man who never bragged and always credited his opponents. That image was a half-truth at best. Greb was as much a tangle of contradictions as anyone else, more so even, though his personality traits—the virtues and the vices—stirred up something that is off by itself in boxing history.

Those who knew him said he *needed* to fight often, that he thrived on "his marathon plan of meeting them all, one after the other." He typically asked for two things—"fair terms" and "the hardest guy" and as a result, negotiations were rarely much more than an offer on one side and a shrug and a signature on the other.

Throughout his thirteen-year career, he was lionized for his "gameness" more than anything else. Exceptional even during an era overrun with folk heroes and iron men, he glowers across a century at celebrity boxers who dilly-dally until a rival ages or breaks down and then swoop in like scavengers, picking at the remains and claiming it as something it is not.

But Greb was too willing.

He went so far as to issue a public challenge to Jess Willard and said he'd donate his purse to the Red Cross. When Fred Fulton fought at Madison Square Garden, Greb was moving with every punch and murmuring that he'd pay $5,000 to fight Fulton that night. He opened negotiations with Luis Firpo, and said he'd fight Harry Wills in an arena or a gym just to prove that the top heavyweight contender in the world wasn't much. All of them towered over him and outweighed him by at least fifty pounds, which suggests that Greb either had screws loose or was a misanthrope raging against all men, including himself.

He was moody, surprisingly vain, and quick to take

offense. If he lost a fight, he was known to call it a frame-up and at times announced his suspicions as facts. If he failed to dominate an opponent, he'd insist on another match and sometimes another and another

Boston Post, 8/25/1919.

to make sure his supremacy was understood.

When a bulletin was posted outside the *Pittsburgh Press* announcing Jim Jab's opinion that he'd lost a fight the night before, Greb happened by and saw it. He ripped it off the board and threw it on the street. Then he went looking for Jim Jab.

In March 1919, he read about Ed Tremblay's contention that he made Greb quit in the King's Tournament and added Greb's name to his record with a "KO 2 rounds" beside it. Greb promised "the beating of his young life for his presumption." Tremblay wouldn't fight him.

After one of his bouts in New York City he went to an all-night joint in Greenwich Village. The morning paper came in and he flipped to the sports section. Westbrook Pegler was there with Red Mason, watching him. "Harry read the stories, moving his lips, then pushed the papers away and sat with his face in his hands." Mason leaned over to Pegler. "His wife's sick," he said. "He's all busted up about it."

"Hey," Greb looked up. "Them bums say I blew a coupla rounds to that guy tonight. What do them bums know?"

In October 1919, the old "White Hope" heavyweight Frank Moran said Greb got a boxing lesson in a recent match, and Greb headed for the telephone. "Now listen," he told the *Daily Post.* "You put a piece in the paper telling Frank Moran that if he really wants to fight, he's looked far enough. I'm his man. What I mean is that he's mine. Size doesn't impress me." Greb posted a grand for a forfeit and his manager was ready to bet that Moran would not only lose big, he would "break ground" when Greb engaged him toe-to-toe. Moran went quiet.

At times he seemed to target siblings—the Chips, the Gibbons—as if on a blood campaign. In the summer of 1912, we can place him in Wheeling, West Virginia for what looks like a spur-of-the-moment professional debut against Young Stoney Ritz. What happened in that fight is a mystery, but he returned to Wheeling twelve years later to fight Stoney's younger brother. In the second round, Greb hit Frankie Ritz with a triple right hand combination that landed Ritz on his back with his feet "tangled grotesquely" up in the ropes. Ritz had to be carried to his corner; Greb walked off "without having disturbed his slicked and glossy hair."

He rarely went down, but if he did, you were in for it. Soldier Buck claimed he knocked Greb down with a right hand and didn't think he'd get up. "But he did—at the count of four. He then proceeded to beat me to death," he recalled. "For two days after the fight, friends had to lead me around. Both of my eyes were closed." There are reports of crowds howling at the referee to stop the carnage when Greb was in one of his sadistic moods, when he sought to prolong punishment out of "pure meanness."

He was just as mean during sparring sessions. While Greb was training for a bout in a New York gym,

Mason invited Jack Sharkey to spar with him. Sharkey, who went on to become the world heavyweight champion in 1932, sent a light heavyweight over instead. Greb felt slighted, got mad, knocked the light heavyweight out, and started taunting Sharkey— "Come on over!"

Roy McHugh described his fighting style as "an uprising of nature." Clouds of rosin dust were kicked up as he tore after any and all, blitzing them to the body and the head, mauling, head-butting, yanking them off balance, ramming them through the ropes, and grinning the whole time. One of his favorite moves was to curl his left glove around the back of a neck and whale away with his right. And he'd laugh off criticism.

In the summer of 1919, he faced a parade of fighters who had no affinity for him, nor he for them. He relentlessly mocked Big Bill Brennan. Battling Levinsky couldn't bring himself to tip his hat to Greb after yet another decisive loss. Knockout Brown and he were "enemies of long standing." There was "bad blood" between him and Mike Gibbons and "the feeling is real," said the *Press*. "Harry and Mike detest each other." Jeff Smith shared a ring with him seven times, which exponentially increased their mutual antipathy. "They hate each other," said the *Daily Post*.

Kid Norfolk can speak for all of them. "That Greb was mean," he said in 1938, and opening his shirt, pointed near his sternum. "See that lump, big as an egg? Greb gave me that with his head. Still sore."

What was driving him? There is evidence of disturbance in the historical record, in the little deaths a fat, crooked-eyed, grammar-school dropout they called "Icky" could be expected to suffer daily; in the choice of a confirmation name that promised violence, in the "wild rage" his father recalled—wild rage that thousands would buy tickets to witness.

Greb became famous for forcing his adversaries— those who would hurt him—backward and on their heels to put himself, the former victim, in control. In other words, his fighting style reflected his psyche. So did his *nom de guerre*. The name "Harry" was adopted at the onset of his career and is assumed to be a loving tribute to a dead brother, but it's more than that. Icky Greb was a frog who imagined himself into a king, and the king had a name. "Harry Greb" was his reconstructed self, the man he aspired to become— fearless, ferocious, and covered in glory.

Memories of his ferocity wouldn't fade for decades. Red Smith couldn't bring up Gene Tunney's name without shuddering at what was done to him by the "bloodthirsty Harry Greb," he said in 1968; by the "carnivorous Harry Greb," he said in 1973.

And yet Greb was always genial toward those who meant no harm. His neighbors on Gross Street liked him for "his sunny disposition." He'd greet civilians with a smile and a warm handshake, and often shared stories filled with Jazz-era slang and devoid of proper grammar. He doled out tickets and whatever else he had in his pockets to the Pittsburgh newsboys who followed him around like his own personal cheering section. When he learned that one of their counterparts in Omaha scaled the wall of an auditorium to watch him fight and fell to his death, Greb sent his parents a check.

He counted many priests among his friends. Father Cox never had to ask twice if he needed him to volunteer at the Lyceum. The late-night knock on the rectory door at Immaculate Conception never startled Father Bonaventure; he knew it was Greb, back from out of town and stopping by with a donation. On Sundays, Greb went to Mass and limited his training to a long walk. He prayed novenas. Before a fight, he would seek out a priest for a blessing on his efforts. "He made quiet little visits to Our Lord in the Blessed Sacrament, asking for aid," said Father Cox, who believed those prayers were answered—"He fought with the courage of a David. He never knew fear and was never tired."

If he lost his temper or wronged someone who didn't deserve it, he would apologize immediately and mean it. He didn't always beat up on opponents. At times he would take it easy on substitutes who couldn't hang with him, and when faced with a situation that would give him an unfair advantage, he'd behave as if a nun from St. Joseph's was watching.

His loyalty is a favorite theme of long-forgotten folk tales. One of them begins with a frantic phone call from Youngstown where a friend had stopped for a drink and was being treated roughly. "Stay right there," Greb said, then sped seventy-four miles north and barged into the saloon. He was still tossing the brute around when the bartender appealed to his friend to make him lay off. "I can't afford to replace this whole joint," he said.

In November 1919, nine-year-old Jack Henry showed up at Greb's training camp in Beaver Falls and was stopped at the entrance. The boy's accent was familiar to Greb. "Are you a Limey, kid?"

"Yes," Jack replied. "And in England they say you're the greatest fighter in the world."

"Let the kid in."

A few nights later, Greb was beating up on Zulu Kid at the Nonpareil A.C. and there's Jack in his corner, in charge of the bucket and sponge.

By the time Greb took Mildred and his contradictions to Conneaut Lake in July 1919 he was at the very least the greatest boxer in his division. But the only thing atop his head was a straw boater hat. He wanted a crown, and Mildred couldn't buy one at The Rosenbaum Company at Sixth, Liberty, and Penn. It wasn't like today—if you were a name-fighter back then the Five Points Gang didn't dangle a belt and a random opponent in front of you for a percentage. And if they did, that era's sports writers would have spotted the sham and shamed it into extinction. Greb had to find a way to get an official shot at the middleweight champion, and that was Mike O'Dowd.

Greb had already defeated two of O'Dowd's predecessors in unofficial bouts, and in 1918 came damn close to defeating O'Dowd himself in what the *Minneapolis Journal* called "one of the most sensational bouts ever fought in the twin cities."

Mason had a master plan for 1919. "Now what I intend to do is have Greb fight every man anywhere near his weight," he said, "and really show who is the best fighter in the middleweight class." He would force O'Dowd to the table.

Things were finally beginning to simmer in July when O'Dowd told the *Gazette Times* he'd be "tickled to death to get a crack at Harry Greb in a bout in Pittsburgh." Other cities were also vying to match them. The *Tulsa World* mentioned that O'Dowd's manager agreed to give Greb a shot at the title and O'Dowd "gave his word." A week after that, a

Mike O'Dowd

promoter in Tulsa said he signed O'Dowd to defend his title against Greb. At the end of July, an athletic association in Toledo said O'Dowd and Greb were set to meet on Labor Day. The *New York Daily News* was among those carrying the story. The problem was no one told Mason, who by then was wringing his hands over O'Dowd's refusal to meet Greb.

On August 5, a matchmaker with the Keystone Club in Pittsburgh was trying to make the fight and flew to New York to meet with the champion and talk him down from the $7500 guarantee he was insisting on. On the 18th there was still talk of Toledo until O'Dowd put the nix on it—"positively refusing" to meet Greb before late in the fall. On the 27th, Greb stepped off the train in New York to meet man-to-man with O'Dowd, who said that he would accept Greb's challenge for September 29 in Pittsburgh if his take was $5,000 with a better than 25% of the gate. It fell through. A promoter in Cincinnati signed Greb to "meet the best opponent he could get on the night of the opening game of the World Series" (later remembered as the Black Sox Scandal of 1919) and tried for O'Dowd. He figured he could do better than the flat fee of $5,000 Pittsburgh offered, but he couldn't, and it fell through.

And so it went. From July through September 1919, promoters in Tulsa, Toledo, Pittsburgh, and Cincinnati all tried and failed to sign O'Dowd to face Greb.

The middleweight king had his defenders though, even in Pittsburgh. Sergeant O'Dowd, after all, was said to be knee-deep in grime in the forest of Argonne during the war while Greb was stationed on a training battleship with a dummy smokestack and wooden guns in Union Square.

"Mr. O'Dowd is quite a man—to be explicit—all man," said the *Evening Tribune*. But Greb made him nervous.

Ed Smith, a Chicago fight critic who refereed Greb-Gibbons II may be the reason why. A story was making the rounds that said Smith spoke with the champion in Toledo just before Jess Willard fought Jack Dempsey, and "solemnly warned Mike that 'if he cared anything for his title, stay away from this fellow Greb.'" In November, O'Dowd faced Mike Gibbons five months after Gibbons lost to Greb. In December, he planned on touring Europe.

Had O'Dowd risked his crown against Greb in 1919, it is very likely Greb would have taken it a year earlier than his wife's deadline, and, given his easy defeat of then-champion Al McCoy, about two years later than he could have. As it happened, Greb's middleweight reign would not begin until 1923—after O'Dowd's successor Johnny Wilson continued the tradition of eluding him for three years plus.

Greb was the *bête noire* of the light heavyweights and his ambitions were unsurprisingly blocked there as well.

Gene Tunney, among the greatest boxers the division ever produced, learned early on that there was something of an abyss behind Greb's dark and deadpan eyes. "He is not a normal fighter," he was told. "He will kill you."

In March 1919, Mason was arguing that Greb was the rightful middleweight *and* light heavyweight champion of the world. He justified it by pointing out victories over Jack "The Giant Killer"

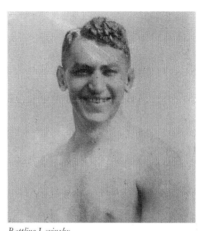

Battling Levinsky

Dillon and his successor Battling Levinsky. At the end of the month, Greb boosted the argument further by beating Billy Miske, another star in the division. The claim was only bluster, but many considered the title lapsed as Levinsky rarely defended it.

In September 1919, Greb demanded a chance and nearly got it.

The Miami A.C. in Dayton, Ohio had signatures from Levinsky and Greb to fight to a decision on the 8th. Greb wired them and insisted that Levinsky make a hundred seventy-five pounds ringside to make sure the crown was up for grabs. The date was switched to the 12th, the 8th, and then back to the 12th before it was postponed until the 15th because Greb was reportedly in a Pittsburgh hospital with boils on the back of his neck. Levinsky, in Dayton on the 12th, headed back to New York. The bout was called off altogether when the promoters couldn't get in touch with him. Did he go on the lam? He never went near Greb again.

Levinsky was, of course, ready to accept a lesser challenge for more money. In October 1920, he defended against "Gorgeous" Georges Carpentier at Jersey City for 20% of the gate minus state taxes. The gate was $350,000 which means Levinsky's take was $65,000. Carpentier had his way with him, knocked him out in the fourth round, and did his part to look like something promoter Tex Rickard could market as a credible opponent for heavyweight champion Jack Dempsey. In July 1921, Dempsey did his part and knocked Carpentier out in the fourth round, also at Jersey City. It was boxing's first million-dollar gate. Carpentier earned a $300,000 purse—over four million today.

Greb could only hang his head.

He'd been trying for a fight with Carpentier since he went overseas during the war. In June 1919 there was talk of a $15,000 purse to meet him in France and in December 1919 Mason was still campaigning for a match in London or Paris.

Greb turned up at Carpentier's training camp in Manhasset, Long Island before the Dempsey fight. Columnist Robert Edgren asked Greb if he'd like to take him on. "Any time," Greb said, "on a day's notice." Later that day the two were introduced and Carpentier, who stood near six feet tall, laughed when he saw Greb, who stood no more than five eight. He'd heard all about this berserker running riot in three weight classes and said he expected a much bigger man. Greb muttered that he was "big enough" and asked him for a match.

Carpentier was friendly, but he wasn't eager. He'd heard too much.

About a week before Dempsey-Carpentier, Greb was rolling his eyes at the French champion's depiction by the press as "a man of destiny" and the so-called secret punch he was supposedly working on at his conveniently closed camp.

He was rolling his eyes again in Billy Lahiff's tavern in New York City when the sports writers' talk turned to Carpentier's chances. Greb broke in. He asked them if they would like to know how good Carpentier was and then invited them to go with him to crash his training camp the next day. "If they let me box him I'll prove to you he doesn't stand a ghost of a chance," he told them. "He can't beat me, much less Dempsey." A huge delegation went with him. Carpentier's manager had a conniption fit. "No! No! No!" he said.

When Greb made Tunney look like a murder scene and took the second-rate American light heavyweight title in May 1922 at Madison Square Garden, Rickard strolled toward the ring as Tunney, "a bloody ruin," was assisted out of it. Rickard told press row that he would offer Carpentier $150,000 to fight Greb for the light heavyweight championship of the world in July. Carpentier's answer? *Mieux vaut prévenir que guérir.*

In June 1922, the AP reported the Frenchman's "unexplained annoyance when the Pittsburgh fighter's name was mentioned." It can be explained now. He saw Greb around every corner, under the bed, in the closet; he saw his shadow on the terrace sipping *noisette*.

In September 1922, promoter Jack Curley was said to be in Paris securing Carpentier's signature to defend his crown against Greb. That was just days before Carpentier met Battling Siki. Fate knocked Greb out of the frame when Siki knocked Carpentier out of his shoes.

Greb could do nothing about fate, though he could do something about Siki. "I will meet Siki anywhere in the world," he said. "Anytime, anywhere." Three offers came in. Greb was revving up when Siki inexplicably agreed to defend against Mike McTigue in Dublin on St. Patrick's Day of all days.

Siki was robbed, McTigue was handed the crown, and Greb was sidetracked again. McTigue, he knew, would keep that crown in a locked box. He had faced McTigue twice already, and McTigue was lucky if he'd won one round in twenty. The first time they met, McTigue's manager was hollering "Hold him, Mike!" from the first through the tenth rounds. "I think McTigue hit Greb once," said the matchmaker. "'Hold him' Mike McTigue is in a class by himself when it comes to holding."

McTigue was tentatively scheduled for a no-decision bout against Greb in June 1923 as a tune-up before facing Carpentier in July. McTigue was set to collect $100,000 to let him try to reclaim the crown and everyone was smiling until Carpentier hurt his hand and the date was postponed. McTigue's manager by then was Joe Jacobs, who surprised him by elevating the Greb no-decision match to a championship match. McTigue made a noble statement about how willing he was to give anyone a shot and then priced himself out of reach.

McTigue lost the crown to Paul Berlenbach in 1925. Greb, middleweight king since 1923, told the *Pittsburgh Courier* that he preferred to face the plodding Berlenbach and become a double champion but was obligated to accept a greater challenge in Tiger Flowers instead.

Two years before Jack Delaney won the light heavyweight crown from Berlenbach, Greb signed to face him and was training hard when Delaney came down with appendicitis and cancelled.

Three years before Jimmy Slattery won the light heavyweight crown from Delaney, Greb beat him in his hometown.

Between 1922 and 1924, Greb went 4-1-1 against Tommy Loughran, Slattery's successor.

In 1925, five years before Slapsie Maxie Rosenbloom beat Slattery to become Loughran's successor, Greb did as he pleased with him and then reportedly returned to the night club where his unfinished highball waited on a table.

Had Battling Levinsky risked his light heavyweight crown against Greb in 1919, Greb almost certainly would have taken it. As it was, he proved himself a master of the division—barreling out of Pittsburgh to face six of the ten light heavyweight champions who reigned from 1914 through 1934. As the smoke cleared, his record against them stood at 16-1-1. Those he didn't face, he chased.

The smoke is still clearing. What comes into view is startling: the greatest light heavyweight who ever lived may have been *a middleweight*.

Jack Dempsey and Harry Greb at Benton Harbor, MI, 1920.

IV. Prohibition Blues

Did Jack Dempsey duck Harry Greb?

On June 30, 1919, American citizens surged into saloons to clink their last glasses of hard liquor, and staggered out. At one minute past midnight on the "thirsty-first," Pittsburgh and everyplace else was subjected to the Wartime Prohibition Act, the "dry law," which was a warmup before the Eighteenth Amendment went into effect in January. Newspapers ran front-page obituaries for John Barleycorn; mock funerals were held in men's clubs, kegs laid out in caskets, whiskey bottles stuffed with black roses. There was an epidemic of hangovers. Many proprietors announced their intention to remain open with the 2.75% beer temporarily tolerated by the Allegheny County DA on tap. No mention was made of crates of ardent spirits stashed in the back; winks went unreported. Over at Epiphany Church, Father O'Connell could have his sacramental wine at Mass and doctors' prescriptions of alcohol for internal ailments would be honored "when the patient is under constant supervision." No refills.

Irish, Italian, and German Americans in the big eastern cities were outraged at this intrusion by blue-nosed busybodies with nothing better to do. At least one Catholic congressman would submit a bill of repeal. "A hard fight looms," said a headline.

A hard fight looms, said the sports section. On July 4, heavyweight champion Jess Willard, who stood six foot six and weighed two-forty-five, would defend his crown against a surging Jack Dempsey. Dempsey, six-one and outweighed by sixty pounds, earned the "Giant Killer" moniker after knocking out Fred Fulton and Carl Morris in a minute or less. He'd been training in Toledo since May. Willard got there on June 30. Both had their life insurance paid to date.

Red Mason, who was handling Pittsburgh's allotment of tickets for the big fight, placed a large bet on Dempsey. Greb, surprisingly, picked the giant.

Both were confident in Greb's chances against Dempsey.

Greb had him in his sights for nearly a year already because of a snub. He was in Philadelphia the previous summer when he heard Dempsey was going to face Billy Miske instead of him. "I think I am entitled to it," he told the *Philadelphia Inquirer*. After defeating light heavyweight champion Battling Levinsky later that night, he was at it again, telling all and sundry that he should get a shot at the man then hailed as the new wonder of the heavyweight class. Then he went and beat Miske in Pittsburgh two months before Dempsey got him in Philadelphia, just because.

"Me for the heavyweight class. I've cleaned up the middleweights . . . and I can go through the light heavyweights just as easily," he said on a train platform in Buffalo in February 1919. "Fight Dempsey, why not? I hope he wins."

Pittsburgh Post, 3/9/1919.

Dempsey turned up in Pittsburgh on March 9 for a week-long engagement at the Victoria. The theater section of the dailies called it "an opportunity to study Dempsey's methods" and Harry and Mildred may have been in the audience doing exactly that.

A week later, Dempsey was asked his opinion about the upcoming Greb-Bill Brennan bout at Duquesne Gardens. He didn't know much about Greb, but he knew Brennan. "He gave me one of the hardest fights I ever had," he said. "If Harry Greb thinks he is going up against an easy proposition in Bill Brennan, he is much mistaken."

"Harry Greb had no trouble in outpointing Bill Brennan of Chicago in 10 rounds last night," said the *Gazette Times* on the 18th.

A tentative deal for Greb-Dempsey went up in smoke after the Willard-Dempsey articles precluded the challenger from boxing anyone before July 4. Another offer materialized for Dempsey to face Greb in an eight-rounder if he beat Willard.

Dempsey brutalized Willard. Meanwhile, Greb was nine hundred miles west of Toledo looking up at Brennan again. No one was confident in Brennan's chances; no one. "There is no telling what is liable to happen to him," quipped one newspaper. Greb "slashed and slammed his way to victory" and took in $1,903.75. It was a fraction of what Dempsey earned.

"Look at that Jack Dempsey. Getting $27,500 for a chance at the heavyweight title," he said. "Say, boy, that's going to be my dish someday. Just watch me."

Connecticut, Cleveland, Philadelphia, Pittsburgh, and Cincinnati made overtures to match Dempsey with Greb. Greb did his part and targeted Dempsey's opponents and sparring partners.

Among the former was Levinsky, whom Greb whipped for the umpteenth time on July 14. Among the latter was heavyweight Terry Kellar, who was running around Ohio claiming Greb was afraid of him. "Greb is no Dempsey," he said. "Those folks who are talking about matching Harry and Jack must want to see the Pittsburgh boy murdered."

"HARRY GREB SLAUGHTERS LOCAL MAN" said the *Dayton Herald* on August 12. "[Greb] won by not more than the length of one of Babe Ruth's really long drives." The crowd had a better time than Greb: "Put some cinders up there so Kellar can run!" "Someone wants you on the telephone, Terry!" "Let him hit you once, Harry!"

Greb was back in Pittsburgh two days later. His next fight was at Forbes Field, which afforded him the novelty of sleeping on a bed with Mildred instead of a railroad bench with Mason. He was looking forward to giving Brennan his fourth consecutive beating when he heard that Brennan was being lined up for a shot at the new heavyweight champion. All he had to do was give "a good showing" on August 23. Greb blew his top. "I'll prevent that meeting," he said. "I'll give Brennan such a lacing that he will not be fit to fight Dempsey or anyone else for many weeks." He also promised to put a decisive end to their one-sided *tête à tête*, and did.

Dempsey gave Brennan a shot anyway. Greb could do no more than delay it, and it wouldn't be the last time he bumped off a prospective opponent only to see him propped back up and given a king's ransom. Brennan extended Dempsey almost twelve rounds before he got stopped. He did unto Dempsey what Greb routinely did unto him—busted him up. Dempsey finished with a swollen eye, a torn ear, and an admission that it was "just about the most closely contested fight I ever had." Greb broke into a wide smile at that and told a reporter that "his idea of a life of ease and comfort would be fighting Brennan once a week for a fair purse, until he retired from the ring because of old age."

Circa 1924. Courtesy of Bill Paxton.

In September 1919, Dempsey's manager Doc Kearns mentioned several fighters in the running for a shot at the heavyweight crown, but was dismissive of Greb. Kearns wasn't alone. In November, after Greb defeated another Dempsey sparring partner, former heavyweight king James J. Corbett forgot all about his own losses to the lighter Bob Fitzsimmons and the smaller Tom Sharkey and scoffed at Greb's chances against Dempsey. "Greb is entirely too light and too small," he said.

Greb found it baffling—Corbett had never even seen him fight. "I think I am as good now as I will ever be, and, without boasting, that I can beat almost everybody in the game, Dempsey not excepted," he said. "I am really anxious to fight him and I do not understand why the fans refuse to consider me in the light of a contender." He then presented his case, listing four contenders Kearns was aiming for: Miske, Willie Meehan, Brennan, and Joe Becket. "I have beaten the first three, each more than once, and would like to fight Beckett," he said. "If, on comparative records, anybody has more license to fight Dempsey than me, I'd like to know who he is."

By early 1920 fans were coming around, especially in Cincinnati, Buffalo, and Philadelphia, where Greb's dominance was witnessed firsthand. There was talk of a ten-round no-decision match to take place in Buffalo on May 31 and reports said Greb hopped a northbound train in January to discuss it with the Queensberry A.C. promoters and agreed to terms. He was in Akron on March 9 when a long-distance call from the promoters came in claiming Dempsey had also agreed to terms.

Greb came home to a mountain of mail, some of it congratulatory, some with sincerest condolences. He had much to say about his stylistic advantages and his intention to win. "I've got everything to gain and nothing to lose," he said, and then asked to be left alone with his thoughts, which were grim. "I'll be in there to do or die," he said. "And I don't expect to die."

In April, Kearns denied that any negotiations had happened. "Bunk," he said, "pure and simple."

In July, Greb got word that Dempsey was in Manhattan, at a training camp at Broadway and Fifty-Seventh Street, and headed to Union Station.

Mason went with him, understandably concerned. A near-peak Dempsey was five inches taller, thirty pounds heavier, hit harder, and was nearly as fast and aggressive as Greb himself. While an official match was a win/win scenario, this was lose/lose. Greb, too willing, thought nothing of risking his health and reputation for zero compensation. And if he did get the better of Dempsey, what then? Would money-mad Doc Kearns risk the heavyweight crown against him? Not likely. It was a crazy idea. Greb didn't care. He would put Dempsey on the spot and show him and the whole world who's who and what's what.

On Tuesday afternoon, July 27, Dempsey looked up and there he was.

Mayhem at Midtown

Reports said Dempsey was "well pleased" when Greb approached with an offer to get into the ring, but this should not be misunderstood. It was no favor from a colleague. It was a direct challenge from an adversary and had to be met.

We don't know what happened on Tuesday except that Greb "boxed four hard rounds" against Dempsey and it got the boroughs buzzing. At three o'clock Wednesday, before Greb came into view, every seat was filled. Outside on 57th Street, a traffic cop had to clear the crowd from blocking traffic.

The price of a ticket was doubled, which meant that for roughly the cost of a haircut and a shave, you could watch David and Goliath—and it was no metaphor. Greb surprised everyone again with his showing, including promoter Tex Rickard and Kearns. Dempsey himself told Rickard that Greb was the first "who ever gave him a real workout."

On Thursday, the added attraction of Douglas Fairbanks acting as honorary referee brought more to the arena door, particularly women. Kearns dubbed it "Ladies' Day" and let them in gratis. We have details about what happened in that last session. "Greb tore into the champion," said one report, "and in the middle of the second round, time had to be called when the Pittsburgher landed a hard right on Dempsey's left eye and split it open." Another report said it was a left hook that blackened Dempsey's right eye. Embarrassed, Dempsey told his handlers he would try it again. A few exchanges later, he told them he would have to call it off for the day.

It was an unofficial TKO. Greb left the ring to ear-splitting acclaim. Fans spilled from the stands and surrounded him.

Dempsey stood by and nursed his eye.

New York fans joined the chorus clamoring for Greb to get a shot at the heavyweight crown. Rickard, who was blocking black title challengers by segregating them into diamond-belt tournaments, did something similar to Greb. He promised him a title shot—at middleweight.

The Battles at Benton Harbor

A few weeks into August, Dempsey's handlers made a hurry-up call to get Greb to the training camp in Benton Harbor, Michigan. Dempsey was said to be concerned about ring rust and news out of challenger Billy Miske's camp that he'd knocked out a sparring partner. This was nothing but hype. Insiders knew Dempsey was doing a favor for Miske, who was sick and watching medical bills pile up to the ceiling.

Greb knew what this was really about. When the two first clashed in July, Dempsey had just finished a stint with a travelling circus—entertaining children with a chimp and champ act and falling in love. This time he'd be ready.

On Tuesday August 31, Dempsey was tearing up sparring partners in a ring set up at promoter Floyd Fitzsimmons's ballpark and promised to continue "hot and heavy for the balance of the week." No one mistook his sun-speckled musculature for rust.

At some point that afternoon, Greb appeared. A fellow middleweight went two rounds one observer said "he'll never forget" and climbed out. As Greb was about to climb in, Dempsey declined. Tomorrow, he said. He'd just gone eight rounds and knew from experience that Greb was not one to tangle with when he's fresh and you're not.

Tomorrow came soon enough. A host of writers were present as time was called and Greb was unleashed. "Greb," went one report, "was in and out, under, around and on top of the champion for the full nine minutes that they traded punches." In the first round, Greb landed a left uppercut and two rights to Dempsey's chin. In the second, he was bouncing around the ring and off the ropes to score punches. "Three lighting lefts" landed on Dempsey's face in the third. It was front page news in the *St. Joseph Herald-Press*.

The *Detroit Times* carried an AP wire that said Dempsey's famous left hooks were missing and he was getting countered to the body and the head and that Greb "gave a spectacular demonstration."

"The Pittsburgher went into him like a hurricane," another wire reported, "piling up points with his rapid, erratic style, and eluding the champion's retaliatory efforts with ease."

Newspapers in the Midwest reported that "Greb staggered Dempsey twice" and the *Chicago Tribune* confirmed that "there was nothing easy about the

Greb (left) "sparring" Dempsey, 1920.

going for either," that it was "a real battle. . . worth the price of admission and more."

The *New York Times* said Greb was "all over him and kept forcing him around the ring"—at times jumping off the canvas to hit him in the mouth—"and seemed to be able to hit him almost at will." It was "a real, honest-to-goodness battle."

Frank G. Menke, one of the foremost sports columnists of the day, said phooey to all that. His coverage opened with a very different tack: "Jack Dempsey doffed the role of slugger today and donned that of boxer and startled the assemblage by his remarkable skill in the new role." It's a curious claim. In other words, the reports of the *New York Times, Chicago Tribune,* and the local newsmen at ringside were the stuff of delusion. Dempsey was merely practicing new shifts, said Menke. He was limiting his offense "to jabs and short wild hooks."

Menke didn't hear Big Bill Tate tell a reporter that Dempsey never pulls punches, that "he just lets them go and when they land—WHAM!" And Dempsey is on record confirming that he was taking no prisoners. "I made up my mind to let myself out today to satisfy myself that I am fit," he said.

Menke's write-up seems to be an attempt to stifle the applause for Greb's showing and his claims were repeated in a letter to the press signed by Dempsey on September 3. It looks like an alibi provided by one friend to another. And friends they were. A few years later, Dempsey bought a racehorse. He named it "Frank G. Menke."

Thirty years later, his friends were still in denial. George A. Barton said Dempsey was handcuffed by Kearns, who wanted him to make Greb look good so he could steal him away from Mason. This too contradicts the contemporary reports; Greb himself swore that Dempsey was trying to knock him out "every day." What's more, at the end of the two rounds, Dempsey asked for one more round, which supports the impression that he "could do little with Greb," looked bad, and tried to save face.

The wide publicity given Wednesday's session brought scores of fans and gawkers in on Thursday. Dempsey seethed all night while Greb weakened his legs with Mildred at a boarding house not far from the camp, and his eyes must have narrowed when he read the front page of Thursday morning's *Herald-Press*: "Newspaper men at the ringside expressed the belief that Greb rocked the champion with a right to the chin in the third round."

When he climbed through the ropes that afternoon, he called on Greb first. One report mentions that eight-ounce gloves were used. Wednesday's were fourteen ounces.

Dempsey "tore into the Pittsburgh lad" immediately, according to the same *Herald-Press*. The *New York Times* said it was Greb who tore into Dempsey and landed a left hook to the body "with all the force at his command." Then "the fur began to fly."

The *St. Louis Post-Dispatch* said Greb "got in some pippins at the start" and as Dempsey returned fire, "the sickening sound of leather smashing flesh echoed around the ball park." Greb was seen eluding Dempsey's left hooks but was absorbing wicked shots to his ribs and there was real concern at ringside that someone might get hurt and badly hurt at that. Kearns was telling Dempsey to "slow down." Mason was telling Greb to "be careful." Greb was mocking Dempsey—"G'wan! Do your stuff champion!"

The UP said Greb "fought viciously all the way" and Dempsey was "soaking Greb hard at long range and in the clinches." *Universal Service* reported that Dempsey "more than held his own" in the first round, Greb hit him flush on the chin in the second, butted him "rather savagely" in a clinch, and then stepped back and was punching him repeatedly at the bell. In the third, Dempsey, spitting blood, went after Greb with body shots that lifted him off the canvas and sent him spinning backward. He was, it said, making Greb miss and countering hard, which is exactly what the AP reported Greb did to Dempsey the day before.

Throughout the match, the two thousand who crammed into the park spontaneously "burst into cheers and prolonged applause." The announcer had to request that they stop exhorting the two combatants—it was too rough already.

Barton rightly framed Thursday's session as Dempsey's answer to the embarrassing coverage around Greb's good showing in Wednesday's session. But his memories about what actually happened were faulty. It was, in his mind, a one-sided rout and much briefer than it actually was. An emboldened Greb, he said, tore into the champion early in the first round only to be immediately paralyzed by "two fearful blows" to the body that popped his mouth open and made a cartoon out of him. Dempsey caught him as he sank and held him up, Barton continued, and Kearns ended the contest early. These details don't appear in the next day's accounts; in fact, a contemporary report said it was Soldier Kelly who he caught under the armpits after a knockout blow.

Barton's memory was faulty; his loyalty was not. He wrote the article in 1952 in response to the "Johnny-

Come-Lately" talk that Dempsey ducked Greb because he was handled in a sparring session. "Let me set you right," Barton wagged his finger. "And don't let anybody tell you differently."

Barton protested too much. His autobiography may tell us why: "The friendship I formed with Jack Dempsey in 1918," he said, "is one that I have treasured down through the years."

At the conclusion of the Thursday session there was bedlam in the stands. The crowd was yelling madly for "more, more," tossing straw hats in the air, and cheering for a full ten minutes. Greb probably made a beeline for Mildred at ringside. Dempsey was sucking wind. A reporter saw him and thought it strange that it should take him so long to recover. He remarked that the champion's conditioning was not what it should be.

But it wasn't that. Dempsey knew what it was.

Greb was in Milwaukee later that September, his spirit as ardent as ever. "I know he cannot put over his famous rights on me," he said. "I would wear him down." "I ask no favors," he went on. "I can make more money in my own class. I merely want to satisfy myself." Mason was bursting with confidence: "We have signed to meet Dempsey, $17,500 our end and if the champion wants any part of our game he can have it any old time."

Dempsey was silent. So Greb tried forcing it again. In June 1921, he went to Atlantic City and took a jitney from Pacific Avenue to Dempsey's training camp with an offer to box, ostensibly to help him prepare for Georges Carpentier. Kearns nixed it. He knew his true intention, which was, said Westbrook Pegler, "to make a fight of it and a spectacle of Dempsey and thus promote himself into the next fight for the championship."

Foiled again, Greb resumed his scorched earth campaign. He went after Kid Norfolk, who was also calling out Dempsey, and Tommy Gibbons, who was deep in negotiations for a shot at the biggest crown in sports. Gibbons simply had to beat "a good man" to clinch the deal. He was foolish enough to sign for Greb.

Thirteen thousand crammed Madison Square Garden, Dempsey and Gene Tunney among them, to watch Gibbons try to win the most important fight of his life with his head stuck in a hornets' nest. Mildred was cheering as Greb landed six and seven punches before pulling away without a return. Jim Jab, who bet on Gibbons, sat awestruck as Greb won twelve of fifteen rounds. Someone yelled, "One more setup for Dempsey is hobbled!" and when the decision was announced, Greb received perhaps the greatest ovation of his life.

Harry and Mildred, circa 1919.

Snippets overheard at the exits saluted the victor, though the very fans who gave him no chance against Gibbons now gave him no chance against Dempsey. He's too undersized they said again. He can't punch hard enough. They're still saying it. Greb heard it then and if he's listening from wherever he is, he hears it today.

He sat in the dressing room with reporters. "I know it is going to make some people laugh but I am positive

I can defeat Dempsey in a 12 or 15-round decision bout." The reporters stopped scribbling and looked up. A few chewed their pencils. "I haven't the slightest fear of Dempsey."

Giant Jess Willard saw and believed. Greb, he said, "is the only boxer who has a good chance to win a decision over Jack Dempsey."

Greb haunted the heavyweight champion like a ghost with soot on his suit. He was in every jitney that pulled into every camp, his voice called him out on sports pages in the name of Bob Fitzsimmons and Joe Walcott, his bland visage was in the bland tea Dempsey sipped with Hollywood fops. Greb was coming at him from every direction, eliminating contenders and targeting sparring partners—men he knew would report back to him. He even shared the name of another Dempsey haunt, but scars on four of the six men Dempsey defended his crown against said Greb, not Wills.

Pittsburgh Daily Post, 2/4/1923.

In April 1922, the *New York Daily News* took Dempsey at his word and invited the fans to decide his next opponent. Harry Wills began and ended the poll with the most votes. Greb spent most of it at third and finished fifth. Al Roberts was third, though Greb knocked him out a week before the poll ended. Kearns and Dempsey whistled right past it; the next opponent was Tommy Gibbons, who placed fourteenth in the poll.

In June 1922, Greb's obsession with Dempsey saw him turn down three offers to fight Johnny Wilson, the middleweight champion. In November he confronted the New York press and rattled off what was becoming, with wins over Gibbons, Tunney, and Tommy Loughran inside of four months, the most remarkable record in boxing history. "If there is anybody else in the field that I have overlooked," he said again, "I'd like to know about it."

He was indeed overlooking others in the field. They'd been staring him in the face the whole time. "I was informed it would be proper for me to give $3,000 to the newspaper men of New York, the money to be used in booming a bout for me with Jack Dempsey," he told a reporter for the *Gazette Times* in February 1923. "I could not see where I should give up my own money for such a project. I fought the proposition for a while, but finally gave up the money under protest." He said too much, didn't say it off the record, and when it triggered an investigation, his denials had zero credibility. This time Greb foiled himself—the boosts he needed stayed in the pockets with the boost money.

Attempts to get Greb the shot were still going on in July 1925, when he was half blind and fighting with his head tilted to the right. Dempsey told Floyd Fitzsimmons that he would sign to meet "anyone except Wills or Tunney," and suddenly Greb's chances got better. Fitzsimmons said Dempsey gave his word. But Dempsey did an about-face and said he needed more time to get into condition. A few days later, he dismissed it outright, claiming that the sole match he wanted was with Harry Wills.

Dempsey never did sign to meet Greb. He never intended to.

Ed Hughes was among those who saw what Greb did to him in New York. "That bout convinced Jack that Greb would be a tough man to beat," he said. Dempsey told Hughes plenty:

> *I'd be a sucker to fight that guy. What would I get out of it? Probably he'd make me look bad for a few rounds. He's a crazy fighter. It would probably take me eight or nine rounds to catch him. And when I knocked him out what would they say? Why simply that I beat a little fellow, and that he made me look bad until I happened to get to him. There's nothing in it for me meeting that guy.*

Instead, he defended his crown against Greb casualties and hype jobs like Carpentier and Firpo. Doc Kearns was no dummy. He saw Dempsey-Greb as a scaled-down version of Willard-Dempsey. When "who's next?" came up as it always did, he ignored the crazy fighter. When cornered, Kearns was shrewd enough to be dismissive. "I don't think Greb would have any chance with Jack," he told Frank G. Menke in 1919.

"Harry Greb could have licked Dempsey," he told Damon Runyon in 1931.

By then, it should be noted, Kearns and Dempsey had parted ways with belligerence on both sides. Even so, Runyon saw a rare moment of candor and zeroed in.

"Oh, you admit then that Greb could have licked Dempsey?"

"Why not admit it now?" Kearns said. "It doesn't make any difference at this late day."

In 1933, the Eighteenth Amendment was finally repealed and Americans, including a few reformed prohibitionists, clinked a glass to ardent spirits. But the damage was done.

Harry, Dorothy, and Mildred Greb. Courtesy of Bill Paxton.

V. Night and Day

Panama Joe Gans proves Greb is just a man and nothing more. Posterity is going to question that.

Harry Greb cast his robe aside and stood in the ring at the Coliseum in St. Louis, "splendidly muscled," noted John E. Wray of the *Post-Dispatch*. It was September 18, 1919. Mildred was heavy with child in Pittsburgh, and Greb had temporarily rested his case to face Jack Dempsey. His opponent wouldn't have heard a word of it anyway; Silent Martin was a deaf-mute bruiser from New York working with a deaf-mute manager who used sign language between rounds.

At the bell, Greb shot out of his corner. "The ring creaked and groaned, and literally shook with the violence of his activity," said Wray, but it was nine months into 1919 and Greb's spirit was finally forcing his body to break ground. Wray saw bandages on his back covering a large boil. There was another one behind his ear.

Boils were plaguing Pittsburgh fighters in 1919. "Those were almost certainly bacterial infections," a nurse told me. "Probably a variety of staph, which thrives in warmth and moisture and was likely passed from boxer to boxer." One of Greb's boils was lanced shortly before the Martin fight, likely the one on his back. That in and of itself was dangerous. There were no antibiotics in 1919 and if the bacteria entered the bloodstream, it could be life-threatening. I asked her if boils were painful. "Big time," she said.

Greb soon had more pain to contend with. Martin, who fought out of a shell and kept his head down, found friends in the officials who would allow Greb no more than a few strips of gauze for his hands, sans tape. In the first round, Greb broke a bone in his right hand "on Martin's head," he said, and yet won every round. In the dressing room, his hand swelled up like a balloon once the glove was removed. The boil behind his ear was also ruptured from a blow, and Greb reportedly got deathly ill that night.

That was Thursday. On Saturday, he was back in Pittsburgh playing handball behind his home on Gross

Bas-relief at Union Station..

Street. His hand swelled up again and Red Mason dragged him to get an X-ray. A photo revealed that the break was clean, "as if it had been chopped with a cleaver." Three upcoming fights had to be cancelled. Greb lost thousands.

On Monday October 13, he took the cast off and probably ran all the way to Union Station for the Philadelphia train, where his opponent proved nowhere near the threat to Greb that Greb was to himself. The price of victory was a rebroken right hand and a piece of bone knocked off a knuckle on his left.

"He is laid up for repairs," said Thursday morning's *Gazette Times*—laid up watching thousands more fly out the window.

On the 16th, Mildred was laid up in St. Margaret's Hospital when something flew *in* the window for a change. It was a stork. Dorothy Mildred Greb, born at 9:15 that night, assured the couple a flesh and blood legacy. It survives to this day in nine direct descendants—two granddaughters, two great granddaughters, a great grandson, and four great-great grandchildren; all but one living in western Pennsylvania.

Greb stood at his wife's bedside with both hands encased in plaster. He needed a little assistance holding his daughter, who shared the name of his sister, his manager's daughter, and his wife and embodied his attachment to those closest to him. Her timing was good—Greb had thirty-two days of something like paternity leave.

Had Father O'Connell counted the weeks between the marriage and Dorothy's birth, he might've found a sin, but on November 15, he stood by the baptismal font with the baby in his arms and a twinkle in his eye. Greb beamed with pride and quite likely peeled off a few banknotes to slip to the priest after the service. Then he was gone again.

Father Lawrence O'Connell

He was training in Canton, Ohio that afternoon and caught a baseball game at League Park. On Monday, November 17 he was at the Auditorium beating

Knockout Brown's face "almost into a pulp." On Monday November 24, he was in a hard fight with a heavyweight at the Southside Market House in Pittsburgh.

Thursday was Thanksgiving. He passed up several large purses for out-of-state matches and did a favor for a small club in nearby Beaver Falls, appearing in the main event after dinner.

Early Friday morning he was headed north to Buffalo, lulled to sleep by the train's rhythmic undulations and the faint sound of station bells passing by.

Soldier Jones was boasting of his plan to put him to sleep too—with "a good solid whack to the jaw."

"How about Greb getting you?" someone from the *Buffalo Morning Press* asked.

"Not Greb," came the reply. "I fought Bill Brennan ten rounds at Quebec and he hit me with both hands plenty and I never even saw stars. I don't think Greb can hit like Brennan and neither do you. If Brennan couldn't drop me, I'm sure Greb isn't going to."

In the fourth round, Jones stood unsteadily and stared at Greb, as if trying to comprehend what was happening. Greb glared back, then proceeded to drop Jones five times, the last on his face where he stayed put. It was Greb's third fight that week, his forty-first without a loss thus far that year.

It is at this juncture, shortly before the end of 1919, that Greb looks to the modern observer as if he's knocking on Achilles' door, never mind Dempsey's.

Two days into December, he stripped away the mythology.

It happened after an Afro-Caribbean welterweight calling himself Panama Joe Gans was introduced at the

Arena A.C. in Syracuse. Gans stood up, acknowledged the crowd, then turned back to his corner and waited. "There was a long wait," said the *Syracuse Herald*. This was the main event and Gans' opponent had yet to leave the dressing room. Gans' opponent was Harry Greb.

Panama Joe Gans

Finally, Red Mason was spotted walking toward the ring with Greb a few steps behind. Greb was in civilian clothes and there was murmuring as they climbed through the ropes. Mason launched into an Arumesque harangue in an attempt to explain why Greb would not be fighting Gans: Gans was the second substitute after the originally-scheduled opponent wrenched his knee. The first substitute couldn't be reached by phone in Jersey City. Gans was one substitute too many. Greb didn't agree to fight Gans. He didn't have to.

Drowned out by hisses and jeers, Mason tried a more direct route and declared that he and Greb had drawn "the color line."

The hisses and jeers got louder.

Greb walked to one side of the ring and awkwardly made an appeal. He admitted that "he wasn't much along that line" and then went and said "niggers."

The crowd's reaction set him on his heels. He heard a word in the din that bruised him—"yellow." The promoter asked Mason and Greb to reconsider and save the main event; the referee encouraged Greb to fight Gans and show "his true sportsmanship." Across the ring, Gans stared at him without a recorded word. Greb was bleeding in his shoes. And still he refused.

As the arena emptied out, Greb said more. It was his wife, he told the *Post-Standard*. He'd made a promise to her "that he would never enter the ring and give battle to a Negro."

It was his wife.

Clannish by culture, Irish Americans had narrow eyes for everyone else, especially the thousands of Southern sharecroppers and field hands buying one-way train tickets to northern industrial centers like Pittsburgh in the 1910s. The Great Migration was not unlike their own flight from home, when waves of peasants broken by the Great Potato Famine left Ireland during the 19th century, crowded into the steerage of ships, and arrived on American shores with nothing but dim hope for better tomorrows. They weren't welcomed either. The Protestant majority saw a threat in their numbers, their poverty, and in the mystical brand of Catholicism they clung to. They huddled in urban enclaves alongside other white ethnic groups to compete in the lowest strata of the economy.

There was one people more despised than they were, and African Americans' later influx into northern urban centers, into the economy, made them competition for decent wages. Their skin color made them an easily identifiable scapegoat. The industrialists, of course, promoted anything that would divide the working class against itself and they were good at it.

Misdirected though it was, the antipathy of first and second generation white ethnic immigrants toward African Americans was spawned in desperation.

The Reillys would have had few interactions with black people; few opportunities for cultural exchange, much less friendship. I found a grand total of one African American in their precinct of Wilmerding borough in 1900—a cook. A few years after Mildred was born, Wilmerding considered itself "fortunate in having few foreigners and negroes of a low type among its population." Black people were the "other" in race-obsessed America, caricatured not unlike the Irish themselves a few generations earlier as gorillas, only without green hats. Mildred, immersed in a race-baiting popular culture, certainly shared a stage with black-faced minstrels and probably laughed along with everyone else.

Greb was raised in a middle-class German household. His influences during adolescence were split between roughhousing friends in Garfield and Father O'Connell's Lyceum, where he was exposed to a wider variety of Pittsburgh's demography. Boxing, more than anything else, would have provided an impetus to overcome his own susceptibilities to race prejudice, to see for himself that the black fighter skipping rope next to him or bleeding in the ring with him was no less a man than he was.

And yet he stood in Syracuse on that December night and casually vilified their race with a slur. This begs the question: was Greb, despite his devotion to an integrated trade, a racist? He might have been. His public use of the slur is an indicator. But the rest of the evidence points to the opposite conclusion.

Someone, likely a reporter for the *Post-Standard* who was familiar with Greb's record, questioned Mason about the whole "color line" routine. Mason conceded that Greb had faced Willie Langford in Buffalo "about three years ago," but said it was due to a misunderstanding. Langford, he said, was a late substitute and Greb battled him because "he didn't want to disappoint the fans at ring side."

Willie Langford.

The truth was Greb faced Jack Blackburn five years before and Langford just the year before. Mason accepted the Langford fight with five days' notice via a long-distance call from Buffalo to Cleveland. Neither Blackburn nor Langford were substitutes; in fact, there was "a storm of applause" from the members of the Queensberry A.C. at the announcement that contracts for Greb-Langford were being drawn up.

GEO. ROBINSON

If Greb had an aversion to African Americans, he had an odd way of showing it. There were four featured on the card that night and after defeating Langford, Greb complimented his skills and then let everyone know he hoped to resume negotiations with Harlem's Kid Norfolk.

In August—at the height of the Red Summer of 1919, when lynch mobs were running amok in the South and anti-black riots was erupting in the North, including eastern Pennsylvania—Greb accepted the challenge of an African American out of Massachusetts. George Robinson was preparing himself for the greatest opportunity of his career and Greb was on a train and on his way when it was called off by Robinson. A telegram came in that said his mother had died.

Panama Joe Gans was a proud and accomplished fighter. When he heard Greb's slur, he stood up with a rebuke—and in so doing reminded Greb that he, Gans, was a man and nothing less. Greb turned to him and apologized. In so doing, he reminds us that he was only a man and nothing more.

His apology would be repeated again and again with more than words.

Greb never did fight Gans, though he soon joined him and Big Bill Tate in Dempsey's training camp. And over the next six years, he met Kid Norfolk, Allentown Joe Gans, and Tiger Flowers on equal terms no less than six times. "Greb fights them all. All sizes all Colors and all Weights," reads a promotional flyer. "Will even tackle a Klu-Kluxer in a Klu Klux City."

His willingness to meet all comers cost him dearly. He lost the vision in his right eye to Norfolk's thumb in 1921, not a half mile from his mother-in-law's house. Mildred may have had a change of heart by that point. Mason certainly did. In 1924, he wrote an open letter to the *Pittsburgh Sun* strongly criticizing Dempsey for sidestepping Harry Wills.

Kid Norfolk

In 1926, Greb's willingness cost him his only world championship and gave Flowers immortality as the division's first black king. Wylie Avenue applauded him because of this. "Our Mr. Greb," said the *Pittsburgh Courier*, "has shown that he is a man among men." The following September, Greb showed up at yet another Dempsey training camp with the same question that Wylie Avenue—that the Wylie Avenues in every city—had been asking for years: "Why don't you fight Harry Wills, Jack?"

But Greb's redemption was yet to come. In early December 1919, he left Syracuse with a dented reputation. He took the Empire State Line to Buffalo, then hoofed it across the platform to catch the Pittsburgh train home. When he at last climbed the stairs and burst through the door at Gross Street, he gathered up Dorothy in his arms, kissed Mildred, and no doubt spoke about the fiasco at the Arena A.C.

On the 10th, he had the first of three fights in three cities over five days. He reinjured his left hand in the first and won every round but one in the next two. Three days before Christmas he was in Philadelphia battling a six-foot Sioux in what turned out to be his last match in 1919. With two rounds to go at the Olympia A.C., he broke the radius in his right arm after one of his wild swings—more or less snapping his forearm in half. Somehow, God knows how, he grit his teeth and gave his opponent "every reason to believe that the world was decidedly an unpleasant place in which to live."

He didn't bother getting his broken arm set until Christmas Eve and the few who knew what happened were sworn to secrecy. "He's stuck around home a lot and hasn't shaken hands with anybody for a long time," said a friend when Greb had been on the lam for weeks.

When business required him to venture downtown, he draped an overcoat over the cast to hide it and probably gazed longingly at Union Station, planning future invasions, brooding over unsettled scores.

Offers to fight so-and-so at this A.C. or that arena kept right on spilling in and it burned him to turn them down. "Food poisoning," the press was told. He had a little indigestion after the Yuletide feast; "not enough to hurt anyone," he admitted later, but it would do.

Why the alibi?

Greb had just made Babe Ruth's new home run record look like schoolyard play.

From January to December he stormed through twenty-one cities in eight states, fought forty-five times, and was on track for well over sixty had scheduled bouts not been cancelled because something—his hand, arm, a boil, or an opponent's nerve—broke. He thrashed five Hall of Famers ten times, personally sought out the middleweight champion in New York City, ran two light heavyweight champions out of the ring, called out Jack Dempsey every chance he got, manhandled heavyweights, and barely lost a round even while suffering unspeakable injuries. And yet at the end of 1919 he's got his cast covered up with his coat and he's hiding in the house for the better part of a month.

Why?

Greb's answer is so bewildering it's funny. "Folks'll think I'm fragile," he said.

Epilogue: The Damned and the Beautiful

There is no train connecting Boston to Pittsburgh without a transfer and a fourteen-hour commitment. JetBlue got me there in an hour and a half.

Twenty miles separate the airport from downtown, twenty miles of super-sized plazas and dual lanes cutting through valleys flecked with gothic stations and converted warehouses. The windows of the 28X bus rattled as it barreled down West Carson Street along the Ohio River, skidding the curb at the base of a virtual woodland wall, the Duquesne incline, as the cityscape and the Fort Pitt Bridge came into view. I was looking for smoke, craning my neck for abandoned mills and blast furnaces left slumping along the banks of the Monongahela. The sun was blazing.

I jumped off the bus on Seventh Avenue and walked to the hotel with the gym bag I use in lieu of luggage over my shoulder. Marriot City Center is at 112 Washington Place, across the street from Epiphany Church, where Harry Greb married the love of his life.

The Marriot stands on the site of the legendary Pittsburgh Lyceum, where Greb spent his adolescence forging what he would become. In 1957, not long before it was demolished, Father O'Connell was still boosting it. All it took to join, he told the *Pittsburgh Press*, "was good character and $4 dues, in that order." Frank Klaus, Fritzie Zivic, Sammy Angott, and Billy Conn were among the world champions who trained there, but Greb was always his favorite. "When Harry came to the Lyceum," he recalled, "Mildred came along and spent her time in the library"—which used to be in the vicinity of the room where I tossed my bag and washed my face. I was surrounded by ghosts. From the window I had a view of the old Union Station. Smoke billowed out from a stack behind it.

The 87 bus takes about twenty minutes to get from downtown to Bloomfield. The site of the house Greb had furnished early in 1919, where Mildred carried hisinfant daughter late in 1919, was easy to find. The address is the same—255-257 Gross Street. There was a baby carriage on the porch. Displayed in a window was an Our Lady of Guadalupe prayer card and a palm branch woven into a cross. I knocked on the door. And knocked again.

In 1921, Mildred was diagnosed with tuberculosis, the third leading cause of death at the time. Greb did everything in his power to return her to health. He bought a bigger house, recruited his sister to care for Dorothy, hired a housekeeper, and eventually moved her to the Adirondack Cottage Sanitarium in Saranac Lake, New York, where he stayed as close as he could as much as he could.

I own an original portrait of the couple that was taken at a Gotham studio in 1922. It reveals much. Greb sits like some Teutonic warlord in a pressed double-breasted suit, eyes blackened, hands abnormally large on his lap. He stares intensely at the lens, as if daring you. Mildred stands beside him pressing a towel to the upper part of his cheek just enough to obscure the misalignment of his eyes. Her face is blood-drained, her stare is blank. There is no trace of the *joie de vivre* I knew she had a few years earlier, no sign of the It girl in earlier photographs.

In mid-February 1923, he brought her back from Saranac Lake to their new home at 6444 Jackson Street. They were barely settled in when threatening letters from parties unknown began arriving, promising all kinds of tragedy for him if he played too rough in his upcoming rematch with New York darling Gene Tunney. Some of them were addressed to Mildred. She contacted the chairman of the state athletic commission with concerns that her Harry was going to be the victim of a "frame-up"; that his American light heavyweight title would be taken away from him— from them. "Harry's title was to her the same as the grocery store to the grocery man's wife," said *United News*. "It was their 'business'."

Tunney-Greb II was broadcast live from Madison Square Garden on the Pittsburgh Post-Westinghouse radio station KDKA. Mildred's fears came true when Harry lost their cherished title on a split decision that looked like a stick-up, never mind a frame-up. It was his first official loss in over seven years.

Mildred's health went into a tailspin; her hacking cough echoing in the house and faintly down through the decades. Greb spent the next three weeks at her bedside or in church lighting votive candles.

On a rainy Sunday afternoon in March 1923, a little more than three weeks after Greb lost to Tunney, Mildred died at home. She was twenty-two years old.

"Was he there?" I asked Jennifer Wohlfarth, his great granddaughter.

"He was home, or trying to get home," she said. "I don't know, but he was never the same after that."

Father O'Connell confirmed this not long before his own death in 1959. "Greb always told me what a wonderful influence she was on him," he said. "After she died he never was the same."

Mildred was buried at Calvary Cemetery on March 21, in a lot owned by Red Mason. Beside her was Mason's five-year-old son who was accidently burned to death in 1918 and his wife, who died in 1919.

On March 31, Greb signed his will and left his entire estate to his daughter. Mason was a witness. It was registered at the Clerk of the Orphans' Court in the City-County Building on Grant Street, which is where Greb applied for his marriage license in January 1919, and where I held both in my hands in 2018.

"He began to fight with more emotion after he lost his wife," Jennifer told me. Always rough, he became rougher still and sparked the ire of fans and writers alike, though Hemingway's typewriter choked with mad glee. "Suppose," he wrote in *Collier's Weekly,* "you had seen the great, crowding, smashing, take it, come in again, thumbing, butting, mean, nasty, bloody, lovely fight he made."

Greb's return bout in Uniontown is telling. The *Morning Herald* said he was "faster and more furious than ever before" and grunting so loudly it was heard all over the arena. He knocked his opponent out cold in the third round and as he lay on his back, Greb snapped out of it. He was seen rubbing water on his victim's head while still wearing gloves. When he opened his eyes, Greb shook his hand, acknowledged the crowd, and disappeared.

I was still knocking on the door at 257 Gross Street when a neighbor snapped me out of it. "They won't answer," she said.

The stained-glass transoms told me the house is old, though it isn't quite a century old. A few minutes' research reveals the house hadn't been built until 1925, which means that it isn't the house the newlyweds moved into in 1919. But I knew who had it built. The real estate section of the *Pittsburgh Press* reveals that a city building permit was issued in June of that year "to Harry Greb for a brick duplex house in Gross st., near Friendship ave., eighth ward." In July 1924 he was granted another permit to build the house that stands next door.

Today, old brick duplex houses similar to Greb's dominate the street, most set back on small lawns, many with striped or forest green awnings peculiarly common in Pittsburgh. The Jolly Roger hung at 208; next door the rainbow flag of the LGBT movement. Both drooped in the heat of a breezeless summer day. A sixty-something black man with trousers hoisted over a potbelly stepped out of his house.

"Ever hear of Harry Greb?" I called out.

"Nope."

"A hundred years ago, he lived down there on the left," I said, pointing. "You should look him up."

"Yep."

Gross Street runs into Penn Ave, which divides Bloomfield from the grittier neighborhood of Garfield. It's lined with cafes and galleries, a few boarded up. I went west and could see the Mathilda Street intersection where Greb confronted Clarence Jackson and literally dodged a bullet. A Botànica is at the corner of North Millvale and the site of the Greb family home is on a decline, hiding behind trees. The family home that stands there now was built in 2005. There's a door mat on the porch—"The City of Champions Welcomes You." I wondered if they knew.

During Greb's youth, Garfield was a working-class neighborhood overrun with second-generation Irish and Germans, though African Americans up from Maryland, Georgia, and Virginia also lived in the immediate area. They were day laborers and Teamsters and sometimes took in boarders—fellow migrants leaving the malicious South behind. A couple and two families, the Blackstons and the Woods, were close neighbors in 1900. Edward Blackston was the same age as Pius Greb and likewise had two daughters and a son. Just around the corner were the Wood brothers, one of them just a year younger than Greb. By 1910, the Blackstons and the Woods were joined by others, including Mathew Crawford and his wife Jennie who were raising four small daughters at 4906 Alhambra Way and sharing their home with Crawford's mother, sister, brother-in-law, and a boarder. A couple with the same surname was at 4914.

Garfield is a predominantly black neighborhood these days. I walked down North Millvale and went east on Broad Street past well-kept and colorful houses with clackety wooden porches. A few were overrun with vines and pitching this way or that with bleached notices on cracked windowpanes. Someone scrawled "black lives matter" on cardboard and stuck it on a fence. At a bus stop a sticker said "eat the rich."

It was past noon and the stifling heat kept everyone indoors. But for the laughter of a few kids in a park and the metallic humming of air conditioners, Garfield was as still as death. I went left on North Fairmount Street, where every step felt like a lunge with Swiss yodeling behind it. Pittsburgh is known for its bridges and rivers but its hills are something else; they made Greb's stamina less of a mystery and had me looking for a bench.

225 Fairmont. Author's photograph.

There's a house looming at 225 North Fairmont, not quite a mile from the family home. Greb lived in it in 1918. I checked the public records later and found out this house was built in 1900, which makes it an historical landmark as far as I'm concerned.

Highland Park is a half-hour walk north from there. I stopped off at Park Bruges, a bistro on Bryant Street, for water and something to justify my place at the bar. A sign across the street said "Jeffrey Smith," I squinted, "Saloon." Jeff Smith. Another ghost. Greb fought him the third of seven times in 1919 and said he had always been "a troublesome customer." He was one of the few adversaries Greb learned to respect; he was also his double in terms of physicality and temperament. Jeff Smith may have had hundreds of unrecorded fights.

When I left the bistro, I got a closer look at the sign. "Salon," it said.

Highland Park was where Greb did his roadwork while a friend drove his Lincoln Coupe and kept pace. I was walking along the serpentine roads when thunder broke the stillness and in a few minutes the heavens split open like a scene from Dante. I ran for cover under an oak tree, drenched and foolish with Brylcreem stinging my eyes, and called for a Zip Trip.

"Ever hear of Harry Greb?" I asked the driver between thunder claps.

Five months after Mildred's burial, in August 1923, he won the middleweight crown she'd always wanted. But he was losing his bearings; his boundless energy, now crossed with sorrow, was like scattershot. He was training in night clubs and chasing chorus girls one after the other and sometimes simultaneously. Paul Gallico of the *New York Daily News* spied him in a joint off Broadway with a sheba on each arm and a highball on the table in front of him. "He was enjoying himself hugely," Gallico said, "and who wouldn't?"

He wasn't. He couldn't take the silence of being alone. He couldn't even sleep without a light on. He moved into a good-time hotel—the Motor Square hotel, where contraband beer was served on the rooftop cabaret (until November anyway, when Prohibition agents seized forty-four barrels stashed in the basement), where fifth floor rooms doubled as gambling dens on any given night (until April anyway, when police raided the rooms and made three arrests).

In December, a loose-lipped friend said he was soon to be wed again, which confirms how desperate he was to fill the void. In late 1924, he became smitten with an eighteen-year-old Methodist performing at the Nixon and approached her, hat in hand, backstage. He was peering through the mists of nostalgia, at Mildred, who appeared at the Nixon a decade earlier and was eighteen when they married. The girl said her name was Louise Walton. Louise was her middle name; her first name, since dropped, was Helen. The Latinized "Helenam" appears as Mildred's first name on her baptismal record.

Louise Walton. Boston Globe 1/5/1925.

Greb was set to marry her within weeks and got as far as a judge's bench when she ran out on him. "The stage is so alluring," she said. "I had to stick." It was reset for a church and then called off again, this time by a priest. Red Mason shook his head; "An opéra bouffe touch to a wedding breakfast in Chicago—with no wedding."

Things got worse in 1925. He and a friend met a couple of floozies at a cabaret on Wylie Avenue, took them to his apartment on North Negley, and were taken themselves in a late-night crap game with loaded dice. The police got involved and Greb, humiliated and not wanting to be taken for a stoolie, tried to push it off. He said he was upstairs asleep.

His hard-fought reputation, so dear to him, was fraying badly. He no longer knew who to even the score with. At times, he flailed blindly. At Highland

Park he got involved in a drunken brawl on one night and on another was in a crowded car when a cop heard a woman's scream and hurried over. The occupants hurled epithets at him and he ordered everyone out of the car. Greb took off running, hailed a taxi, and sped off. The cop commandeered another one, gave chase for four miles, started shooting, and Greb was halted and arrested for disorderly conduct. Everyone was due in Morals Court the next morning, but none showed up and their $30 bonds were forfeited. Greb probably reimbursed them himself to keep the incident quiet. It made the newspapers anyway.

On February 26, 1926, Tiger Flowers outspeeded him, forced him to break ground, and took his beloved middleweight crown at Madison Square Garden. When the decision was announced, Flowers jumped three feet into the air. Greb bowed his head and cried. "He was the personification of tragedy," said the *Brooklyn Daily Eagle.* In May, a chorus girl named Sally Bronis hit his reputation harder than Flowers hit his chin when she went public about their stormy little affair. "He said that he was enthralled with my beauty and began his ardent suit then and there," she said. Did he propose? "That's all he did." There's a certain glee in her claim that he told her manager to "add some cloth to her costume," that he asked her "to be a mother to Dorothy," and especially in what she said about his pleas to tear up his sappy letters and telegrams: "Of course I never did."

It was revenge. Greb's main squeeze was Naomi, but Sally and Louise were competing at the sidebar. Greb chose Louise, kept Naomi in the dark, and scorned Sally who sued him for $100,000—for breach of promise to wed.

Sally Bronis
Daily News (NY), 10/23/1926.

Enter Sally's husband, exit Sally and her suit. He had a heart that needed mending too, so he sued Greb for $250,000—for alienation of affections.

On August 19, while Greb was getting ready for the rematch against Flowers at the Garden, a man approached. "Something for you," he said, and handed him a summons on behalf of Sally's husband.

Greb lost another split decision. "I don't know what I am going to do," he said.

On September 16, he faced a nightmare he'd been putting off since 1921. His dead right eye had to be removed to arrest the rapidly worsening condition of his left. It was either that or total darkness for the rest of his life. But the loss of his eye ended his career, his reason for living, and the darkness came anyway.

Exactly one week later, Dempsey defended the heavyweight championship of the world against Tunney in Philadelphia. Greb was seen sitting ringside in the rain with a black patch over his right eye—over a secret he hoped never got out. "Cataracts," he said. He watched in private turmoil as his archrival defeated Dempsey and won the glory he'd coveted for seven years.

Despair set in. His brother-in-law said he lost his spirit and was having premonitions of death.

On Sunday October 10, he was speeding over the West Virginia-Pennsylvania state line when his car careened over an embankment and flipped several times. Jack White, his secretary, broke his arm. "When I got to Harry," White said years later, "he was pinned in against the wheel and had broken the bone near his eyes." Greb, self-protective to the end, refused treatment and sought to keep the accident out of the papers.

The next Saturday, he threw a seventh birthday party for Dorothy and spent most of the time playing with the children. Few knew he was suffering from excruciating headaches; only later was it discovered that the impact of the crash fractured a bone near the base of his skull. It was "pressing against his brain," White said, and he would pace his apartment, punching the walls because of the pain.

On Wednesday morning October 20, the front page of the *Pittsburgh Daily Post* announced that Tunney was due in Saturday as an honored guest of the city, of *his* city. Excited chatter was everywhere; on the streets, in the speaks, outside the smoke-belching mills along the rivers, at Union Station, in Garfield.

Deeply troubled, Greb left.

He headed to a private sanitarium in Atlantic City to see Dr. Charley McGivern, a long-time friend. McGivern examined his injuries and Greb was reportedly told he had little chance of survival if he consented to an operation, but he'd be dead within six months if he didn't. "Greb knew he was going to die," said sources close to him and the surgeon.

On Friday, the morning after the operation, he fell into a coma. His last battle was waged in the hush of a hospital room as his breathing slowed and eventually tapered off into sporadic gasps. It was raining outside when his great heart stopped.

A beautiful woman cried at his bedside. She looked like Mildred.

The morning sun was just beginning its climb and I was on a bus barreling east on Second Avenue along the Monongahela River. Calvary Cemetery straddles the Greenfield and Hazelwood neighborhoods and is fifteen minutes from downtown. I jumped off at the end of Greenfield Avenue and passed between its iron gates looking for section W. Behind me, in the increasing distance, was the hum of Pittsburgh on the way to work, of iron and steel and smoke and industry, of speed.

I found Harry Greb's headstone high on a hill.

That's all it says—*Harry Greb*. There's no mention of his reign as middleweight king, or his status as the one man to defeat Gene Tunney, or the pandemonium of 1919. There's nothing to persuade historians that Red Mason was right, that we'll never see his equal in the fistic world. He left us with only his name, engraved on a headstone high on a hill.

He isn't alone. Before he died, he asked that Mildred's remains be exhumed and reburied beside him when the time came.

And there she lay, close enough to hold his hand.

ſources and Acknowledgements

I. This Side of Paradise

Harry Greb's insistence on a Solemn High Mass recalled in *Pittsburgh Daily Post* 1/31/1919 and *Pittsburgh Gazette-Times,* 1/28/1957. The complete folk rhyme alluded to is as follows:

Married on Monday, married for health.
Married on Tuesday, married for wealth.
Married on Wednesday, the best day of all.
Married on Thursday, married for losses.
Married on Friday, married for crosses.
Married on Saturday, no luck at all.

Information regarding Harry and Mildred's marriage in County of Allegheny Department of Court Records, specifically the Wills/Orphans' Court Division Application for Marriage License and Consent in the Marriage of a Child or Ward dated 1/25/1919, and the *Daily Post* 1/7, 26, 29, 30, 31/1919. Mildred's shenanigans found in *Daily Post* 8/5, 12/15/1915, *Gazette-Times* 8/15/1915, and *Pittsburgh Press* 12/14/1915. A girl of her approximate age appears in the 11/8/1909 edition of the *Daily Post* after a teacher in Butler, PA was brought before the school board for whipping two girls, one of which was "Mildred Riley" and whom the teacher was having much trouble handling due to their rough play. Mildred was a chorus girl; this is confirmed in *Daily Post* 1/21/1917, *Pittsburgh Press* 3/27/1919. Reilly family background reconstructed from U.S. Census repots, birth records, city directories, reminisces of Red Mason found in *Gazette-Times* 11/8, 9, 10/1926; phone conversation with Jennifer Wohlfarth 6/29/2018; Marriage Certificate of Thomas Reilly and Bridget Beatty, dated 11/20/1899; Indiana State Board of Health Certificate of Death for Thomas J. Reilly filed 8/27/1907, and Pennsylvania Department of Health Certificate of Death for Irene Reilly filed 11/13/1934. Victoria Theater described in *Daily Post* 8/1/1913. "Be-Brite" campaign in *Pittsburgh Press* 4/15, 5/4 and 8/11, 12/1915, and *Gazette-Times* 4/29 and 8/15/1915. Mildred was also reportedly employed as "a long-distance operator for the Bell Telephone Company" before her engagement (see *Pittsburgh Post* 1/7/1919). [*Note*: Mildred's descendants believe that she was a beauty queen; I found no evidence of that, though there was a beauty contest in Pittsburgh, sponsored by the *Pittsburgh Press* in the spring of 1915. Hundreds sent in pictures and there were ten finalists in the Western Pennsylvania, Eastern Ohio, and West Virginia region. Mildred's name was not among them. Her interest, however, would be almost ensured by the prize—a luxury train trip to Universal City, California with a promise of a debut as a movie star.] Parish/Sacramental records of Eduard Henry Greb and Mildred Reilly courtesy of Dennis Wodzinski and Suzanne Johnson of the Diocese of Pittsburgh's Archives and Records Center. Lillian Elizabeth Greb's Pennsylvania Bureau of Vital Statistics Certificate of Death filed March 27, 1908; date and details of Greb's confirmation in *Daily Post* 5/11/1908. Pius Greb's recollections in *Shamokin News-Dispatch* 10/21/1944. [*Note:* Greb claimed that his mother was Irish while his biographers claim that he is of German stock on both sides. There's a chance, however slim, that his ancestors immigrated to Germany from elsewhere and insulated themselves. His great granddaughter Jennifer Wohlfarth reports no trace of Western European blood. Her DNA is predominantly Scandinavian (31%), Irish (23-42%), and Italian (15%), the latter of which may explain her (and Greb's) dark features— who knows, it may also explain Greb's penchant for vendettas.] Greb's sixth-grade education was told by Red Mason to Havey Boyle in *Gazette-Times* 11/9/1926. Other information derived from that series are his personality traits as a child, school difficulties, leads to where he found employment, hijinks, Rabbit Smoots, the Wheeling debut, and the Cumpston bouts; details also found in *Gazette-Times* 10/23/1926; Greb's boyhood "pet names" were hollered at him during a fight recounted in the *Pittsburgh Press* 1/26/1915; his awkwardness described by Father Cox in *Gazette-Times* 10/26/1926. His lazy/cocked eye can be seen in several photos before the first Kid Norfolk fight in 1921 where his right eye was injured; Cuddy DeMarco recalled it in *Pittsburgh Press* 10/22/1946 and also comments on his vanity as does Gene Tunney in numerous sources. Regis Toomey's recollections in *Pittsburgh Press* 6/1/1961; his sister Ida reveals origin of "Icky" nickname and tells us that he was "fat as a butterball" and literally ran to work at Westinghouse every morning in *Pittsburgh Post-Gazette* 3/20/1947. Father O'Connell's Lyceum and parish discussed in undated (circa 1990s) articles found in Harry Greb file at Carnegie Library of Pittsburgh; see also Roy McHugh's article in *Pittsburgh Press* 1/28/1981 and Father James Cox's sermon in *Gazette-Times* 10/26/1926. [*Note*: In the summer of 1912, Greb and a friend who did not laugh at his aspirations hopped a train to Wheeling, West Virginia and, the story goes, Greb talked his way into a six-rounder against Young Stoney Ritz at the Moose Club, earning enough for fare home. Greb's presence in Wheeling in 1913 in "an exhibition" at the Moose Club on Union Street was corroborated in the *Wheeling Intelligencer* 2/27/1915. "Young Stoney Ritz" was John Michael Ritz and he later became a boxing instructor and promoter. Greb also fought Ritz's younger brother Frankie in 1924, as seen later in the story. Frankie became an ordained minister and pastor at the First Christian Church in Vanderbilt, PA after retiring from the ring. Both were sons of Judge John Stonewall Jackson Ritz. The second Red Cumpston bout, fought after the Cleveland amateur tournament on 4/5/1913, does not appear to be a professional bout. It was announced in the *Pittsburgh Press* on 4/4 as part of "a boxing show" put on by Hampton Battery B of the National Guard, at Armory hall in Pittsburgh. "Harry Grebbs, amateur 145-pound champion, vs, Red Cumpster, who took second medal in the same class" is listed in the middle of several other bouts, most of which include not where the fighter hails from, but the club they represent. This detail, as well as the fact that there seems to be no report of the results, point toward the match being an amateur contest. Greb says he was offered $12 for the bout and that would technically make it a professional bout; Mason also considered it a professional bout though he may be simply parroting Greb's recollection as he was not managing Greb at that time. Greb also said he knocked Cumpston out in the second round that night, which is inaccurate. Greb fought Cumpston again a month later and knocked him out in the third round. Was that one a professional bout? The referee called it "a smoker" (see *Pittsburgh Press* 5/12/1913) though that tells us nothing. The most likely scenario may be that this, the third match between Greb and Cumpston in which Greb (called "Krebbs" in the account) knocked Cumpston cold, was indeed a professional bout and that Greb was paid $12 for it.] The Clarence Jackson incident and context assembled from *Daily Post* 9/27, 28, 10/8, and 11/24/1915; *Pittsburgh Press* 11/24/1915, 4/23/1907, and 12/20/1916; *Gazette-Times* 9/27/1915. Pre-fight "exchange" between Greb and George Chip bout *Pittsburgh Daily Post* 10/6/1915. Naval reserves information derived from the military records of "Harry Edward Greb" from National Archives, National Personnel Records Center in St. Louis, MO (postmarked 11/8/2018); see also *Daily Tribune* (Wisconsin) 3/28/1918, *Evening News* (Wilkes Barre) 5/9/1918, *Pittsburgh Daily Post* 7/28, 10/21, 11/21/1918; *Buffalo Enquirer* 12/13/1918, and *Plain Dealer* 12/26/1918. England tournament recounted in *Reno Evening Gazette* 1/18/1919. London street fight in *Arkansas Democrat* 1/23/1919 and *Cincinnati Enquirer* 1/26/1919. Information about Pittsburgh during this time is found in *It Might Have Been Worse: A Motor Trip from Coast to Coast* by Beatrice Larned Massey (Kessinger Publishing, 1920) and *Pittsburgh, How I See It* (1916). "Hell with the lid [taken] off" is James Parton's famous quip about Pittsburgh and appeared in *Atlantic Monthly* in the January 1868 issue. "Anybody, anywhere, anytime" is in *Gazette-Times* 7/8/1939 though variations of this declaration are found all over the place. I read several books including *1919: The Year Our World Began* (1987 © William A. Klingaman), *1920: The Year That Made the Decade Roar* (2015 © Eric Burns), *The Night Club Era* (1933, 1960 © Stanley Walker), *Daily Life in the United States 1920-1940* (2002, 2004 © David E. Kyvig), and *The Damned and the Beautiful: American Youth in the 1920s* by Paula S. Fass (1977 © Oxford University Press) for background and context.

II. I'd Go a Long, Long Way for You
Wedding reception covered by Harry Keck in *Pittsburgh Daily Post* 1/31/1919. "Rip Roaring" Tommy Robson was the reason why Greb was late to his own wedding—warning bells rang louder than wedding bells that morning, so instead of suiting up with his best man, he was sprinting around Highland Park in below freezing temperatures; details in *Daily Post* 1/29/1919, *Buffalo Commercial* 1/29/1919, *Plain Dealer* 2/1/1919, *Akron Evening Times* 2/1/1919, *Boston Herald* 2/10/1919. Robson's statement in *Harrisburg Telegraph* 2/10/1919. Descriptions of Greb's style in Grantland Rice's Sportlight column 12/26/1940, *St. Louis Star and Times* 9/11/1919, *Buffalo Commercial* 5/21/1919, "pandemonium" in *Evening News* (Harrisburg, PA) 4/8/1924. Letter in *Cincinnati Enquirer* 10/21/1917. Home furnished in *Daily Post* 1/26/1919. Set-up critique in *Pittsburgh Gazette-Times* 2/5/1919. Brennan I in *Buffalo Commercial* 2/12/1919 and *Daily Post* 2/11/1919. Levinsky bout in *Gazette-Times* 5/23/1919, *Pittsburgh Press* 2/17/1919, *Buffalo Courier* 2/12, 18/1919, *Buffalo Morning Express* 2/19/1919, *Buffalo Enquirer* 2/12/1919, *Buffalo Commercial* 2/18/1919. Quip about cops in *Daily Post* 2/20/1919. Information about Chuck Wiggins in IBRO's "Chuck Wiggins King of the Back Ally Brawlers" by Robert Carson (2/1/2008), *Detroit Times* 3/4/1919, and *Pittsburgh Press* 5/19/1942. Houck fight in *Pittsburgh Press* 3/7/1919. See also *Repository* 4/21/1919. "[F]ights all day" in Ed Harmon's "Around the Bags" in *Daily Illinois State*

Journal 6/30/1919. "One Round" Davis bout in *Buffalo Commercial* 4/8/1919, *Buffalo Enquirer* 4/7/1919. Robson again in *Daily Post* 5/27/1919. Joe Borrell bout in *Gazette-Times* 6/19/1919, *Jackson Daily News* 6/17/1919, and *Evening Public Ledger* 6/17/1919. Mike Gibbons rematch in *Gazette-Times* 6/23/1919, D.J. Tice's article in Tom and Mike Gibbons Preservation Society, 6/27/1999, *Pittsburgh Press* 6/13/1919. Keck's comments about inhuman/superhuman in *Gazette-Times* 6/27/1919. Greb on train from Wheeling to Pittsburgh in *Gazette-Times* 6/22/1919.

III. The Uncanny
Roy McHugh's letter to author regarding Mike Gibbons, dated 8/21/2015. Details around Gibbons II in *Pittsburgh Press* 4/4, 6/15, 17, 18, 24/1919; *Pittsburgh Gazette-Times* 6/22/1919; Barton's recollections in *My Lifetime in Sports* (© 1957 Stan W. Carlson) pp. 62, 65; *Cincinnati Enquirer* 3/6/1919. Joe Chip bout covered in *Gazette-Times* 7/24/1919, *New Castle Herald* 7/25/1919 (see Bob Randall's observation about use of head and hitting in clinches and Red Mason's teachings), and *Daily Post* 7/25/1919. Conneaut Lake in *Gazette-Times* 7/28/1919, *Press* 8/10/1919. *Morning Herald* (Uniontown, PA) 6/18/1919. Greb needed to fight often to stay sharp in several sources including *Pittsburgh Press* 12/14/1919 and *Daily Post* 7/31/1921. While in Cincinnati on 12/18/1917, Greb announced that he was "ready to fight Jess Willard, world's heavyweight boxer, and agreed to meet the champion

on his own terms, and give the entire receipts to the Red Cross" (*Boston Globe* 12/19/1917); see *Gazette-Times* 12/1/1919 and Robert Edgren's column on 3/3/1922 for Greb's urge to fight Fred Fulton; see also *The Times-Bridgeport Evening Farmer* 12/15/1919. Ready to fight Luis Firpo in *Morning Herald* 6/18/1923. Willing to fight Wills in *Gazette-Times* (4/24/1925). Personality traits derived from numerous sources including *Tacoma Daily Ledger* 1/10/1924, *Gazette-Times* 6/23/1919, and *St. Louis Star and Times* 9/11/1919; described as "moody" and "truculent" in clipping found in Greb file at Carnegie Library. "Greb stands ready to tackle anyone who questions his superiority" in *Denver Post* 9/11/1921, and Greb's being out to prove he is the superior fighter in *Pittsburgh Press* 3/26/1919. "The few times he actually lost in his career, he refused to believe that he had been worsted" in *Gazette-Times* 10/23/1926. Interpersonal issues in *Pittsburgh Press* 3/10/1946, 4/30/1954, and 3/20/1919; *Times-Bridgeport Evening Farmer* 6/18 and 10/10/1919, *Daily Post* 3/23, 31/1919; *Chicago Tribune* 11/21/1926; *Daily Post* 10/16/1919, *Pittsburgh Press* 10/23 and 11/3/1919, *Duluth News-Tribune* 10/24/1919; *Gazette-Times* 11/9/1926, *Wheeling Intelligencer* 2/27/1915, *Daily Post* 11/26/1924, *Wheeling Intelligencer* 11/26/1924; *Courier-Journal* (Louisville) 7/7/1963; *Gazette-Times* 7/13/1919, *Daily Post* 9/20/1919, *Pittsburgh Press* 6/16/1919; "laughing off criticism" in *NY Daily News* 2/15/1923; "an uprising of nature" is in *Pittsburgh Press* 11/17/1968; incident with Jack Sharkey in *Pittsburgh*

Press 1/28/1930; Kid Norfolk's lump in *Charleston Evening Post* 2/25/1938; Red Smith in Publisher's Hall Syndicate 11/4/1968 and *New York Times News Service* 8/8/1973. "Sunny disposition" in *St. Louis Star and Times,* 9/11/1919. Newsboy who fell to his death in *Columbus* (Nebraska) *Telegram* 2/8/1926. See also *Gazette-Times* 11/20/1926. Bernard "Happy" Albacker quoted in *Pittsburgh Press* 10/22/1946, *Morning Herald,* 6/18/1919. Father James R. Cox was the director of the Lyceum (*Pittsburgh Press* 3/21/1915) and recalled Greb's Catholicism in a radio sermon (transcript in *Gazette-Times* 10/26/1926, see also *Daily Post* 10/28/1926). Father Cox was also the so-called "Shanty Priest" who went on to national fame as the head of "Cox's Army" and as a candidate in the presidential race of 1932 for the wonderfully-named Jobless Party. Jack Henry's story told by Roy McHugh in *Pittsburgh Pot-Gazette* 8/19/1995. Greb after middleweight crown and Mike O'Dowd: *Pittsburgh Press* 1/2/1919, *The Times-Bridgeport Evening Farmer* 4/24 and 6/14/1919, *Watertown Daily Times* 6/13/1919, *Gazette-Times* 7/4, 8/5, 8/27, 9/22, 9/12, 9/15, 12/4/1919 *New Orleans States* 7/11/1919, *Detroit Times* 7/24/1919, *Daily Post* 7/31/1919, *Seattle Daily Times* 7/31/1919, *NY Daily News* 8/1/1919, *Altoona Tribune* 8/2/1919, *Tulsa World* 4/1, 4/27 and 8/4/1919, *Miami Herald* 8/18/1919, *Pensacola Journal* 8/22/1919, *Evening Tribune* 8/22/1919, *Repository* 8/27/1919, *Patriot* 9/10/1919, *St. Louis Star and Times* 9/11/1919, *Denver Post* 9/12/1919, *Daily Post* 11/20/1919, *Philadelphia Evening*

Public Ledger 11/21/1919, *Evening Tribune* 8/22/1919, *Denver Post* 11/26/1919, *Gazette-Times* 8/7/1919. Tunney recalled being warned about Greb in *Pittsburgh Press* 3/23/1963. Greb after light heavyweight crown and Battling Levinsky: *Tulsa World* 4/1/1919, *Pittsburgh Press* 3/27/1919, *Dayton Herald* 8/29, 9/1/1919; *Dayton Daily News* 9/3, 10/1919; *Pittsburgh Press* 9/7/1919, *Gazette-Times* 9/4, 12, 15/1919; *Plain Dealer* 9/13/1919, *Daily Post* 3/28, 9/16/1919. Greb's pursuit of Georges Carpentier: *Gazette-Times* 12/29/1919, Robert Edgren interview 10/29/1921, Barton's *My Lifetime in Sports,* p. 101-102; Davis J. Walsh, International News Service 5/24/1922; Damon Runyon 10/26/1922, AP 6/23/1922. *"Mieux vaut prévenir que guérir"* more or less means "better safe than sorry." Regarding Siki: *Boston Daily Globe* 9/27/1922, *Daily Post* 1/17/1923. Regarding McTigue: *Daily Post* 12/13/1919, *San Francisco Chronicle* 2/14/1919, *Buffalo Morning Express and Illustrated Buffalo Express* 6/12/1923, *Daily News* 6/12/1923 and *Rochester Democrat and Chronicle* 6/12/1923. Regarding Berlenbach: *Pittsburgh Courier* 1/9/1926. Regarding Delaney: *Republican and Herald (Pottsville PA)* 3/14/1924, *NY Daily News* 6/11/1924. Matt McGrain ranked Greb #3 in his light heavyweight countdown "The Fifty Greatest Light Heavyweights of All Time," which was published on the TheSweetScience.com, 6/15/2015. McGrain is an authority and therefore boosted my confidence in writing the final sentence of this section.

IV. Prohibition Blues

Prohibition "warm up" in *Pittsburgh Post* 7/1/1919. Life insurance paid in *Evening Tribune* 6/12/1919; tickets and bets in *Pittsburgh Gazette-Times* 5/19 and 6/29/1919; "one ambition" in *Evening Public Ledger* 7/14/1919; Greb targets Dempsey *Philadelphia Inquirer* 8/6/1918 and *Scranton Republican* 8/12/1918. Dempsey at Victoria reported in *Pittsburgh Press* 3/4/1919, *Gazette-Times* 3/18/1919; Brennan in *Pittsburgh Press* 3/15/1919. Tentative Dempsey-Greb *Buffalo Courier* 2/17/1919, *Denver Post* 7/2/1919; Greb-Brennan III *Bridgeport Evening Farmer* 7/4/1919. Greb on Dempsey purse *Buffalo Courier* 2/13/1919. Attempts to make Dempsey-Greb in *Gazette-Times* 9/8/1919, *Bridgeport Evening Farmer* 7/16/1919, *Gazette-Times* 7/21, 22/1919; *Repository* 8/15/1919, *Harrisburg Telegraph* 2/18/1919, *Dayton Herald* 8/5/1919. Kellar on Dempsey-Greb *Dayton Daily News* 8/6/1919; Greb-Kellar II: *Dayton Herald* 7/19 and 8/4/1919, *Dayton Daily News* 8/10/1919, and *Dayton Herald, Gazette-Times, Pittsburgh Press, Jackson Daily News* 8/12/1919. Greb riled over Brennan in *Pittsburgh Press* 8/8, 13/1919; fight in *Gazette-Times* 8/24/1919. Robert Edgren interview, 10/29/1921. Dempsey gives show business a try in *Detroit Times* 7/26/1919, *Dayton Herald* 8/9/1919, *Scranton Republican* 7/10/1919, *Gazette-Times* 9/22/1919, *Bridgeport Evening Farmer* 9/24/1919. Corbett comment in King Feature Syndicate 11/30/1919. Greb anxious to fight Dempsey: *Gazette-Times* 8/7/1919. Dempsey-Greb in Buffalo discussed by John E. Wray in *St. Louis Dispatch* 1/21/1920, *Gazette-Times* 2/8 and 3/14/1920, *San Antonio Evening News* 3/10/1920, *Evening Public Ledger* 2/4/1920, *Anaconda Standard* 3/19/1920, (Bat Masterson quoted in) *Dayton Daily News* 3/24/1920, and *Buffalo Enquirer* 4/3/1920. "Mayhem in Manhattan": *Daily Post* 7/28, 30, 31/1920, clipping 7/28/1920 "Greb and Dempsey Workout," and *Boston Post* 7/31/1920. "The Battles of Benton Harbor": *Pittsburgh Daily Dispatch* 7/28-30/1920, *Salina Daily Union* 8/25/1920, *Press and Sun Bulletin* 8/28/1920, *Salt Lake Telegram* 8/29/1920; *Detroit Times* 9/1, 3/1920; *Fort Worth Star-Telegram* 9/1/1920, *Chicago Tribune* 9/2/1920, *Duluth News-Tribune* 9/2/1920, *Daily Illinois State Register* 9/2/1920, *Herald-Press* (St. Joseph) 9/2 and 3/1920, and *Pittsburgh Daily Post* 9/2/1920. Dempsey said Greb was talking at him during one of their matches; this was found in *Pittsburgh Press* 4/25/1926. Menke's version in *Universal Service* 9/2, 3/1920; see also *United Press* 9/3/1920, *Anaconda Standard* 9/3/1920, *Arkansas Gazette* 9/3/1920, P.T. Knox for *New York Times Service* 9/3/1920, *Muskegon Chronicle* 9/3/1920, *St. Louis Post-Dispatch* 9/3/1920; Dempsey's letter dated 9/3/1920. Hype Igoe's column included Greb's claim about Dempsey going for the knockout "every day" (6/4/1922). Barton's claims about Dempsey-Greb in *Star-Tribune* 5/11/1952, friendship with Dempsey in *My Life in Sports* p. 89. Dempsey "caught Soldier Kelly under the armpits" during sparring in *News-Palladium* 9/2/1950; reconstructed report by Gregg Perry from accounts from that paper during that time and the *New York Herald-Tribune*. Greb tried fighting Dempsey again before Carpentier fight in *Chicago Tribune* 11/2/1928. Greb's "ardent" spirit in T.S. Andrews in *Dayton Daily News* 10/30/1920; see also Robert Edgren interview, 10/29/1921; *The Lost Journalism of Ring Lardner* (editor: Ron Rapoport; 2017 © The Board of Regents of the University of Nebraska) p. 293; *Gazette-Times* 6/29/1921. Greb conversation with Dempsey in *New York Times* 8/27/1926; Dempsey on Greb in *Pittsburgh Press* 2/19/1922. Gibbons fight at MSG *Pittsburgh Press* 3/22/1922, *Hutchinson Gazette* 3/18/1922, Billy Evans column 3/18/1922, 6/12, 22/1922, 11/10/1922— Greb became, or should have become Dempsey's logical contender after this victory. Willard for Greb against Dempsey AP 9/20/1923. [*Note*: In 1919, Tommy Robson said only Dempsey can stop Greb but had second thoughts in 1920, "[B]elieve me," Robson said then, "he'll give Dempsey a mighty interesting fight despite the fact that he's shy about 15 pounds in weight. He would have Dempsey tied in knots taking punishment. Dempsey might get him, but I think Greb would give Jack a tough battle" (*Cincinnati Post* 12/7/1920).] Greb's letter in *Pittsburgh Press* 3/22/1922; skips Johnny Wilson *Boston Herald* 1/10/1922. Complaint to press about being overlooked again (11/25/1922). Greb told Charles J. Doyle of the *Gazette-Times* about the "boost money" he gave to NY writers; Greb's later denial that he said what Doyle said he said rings hollow. Fitzsimmons and

Dempsey *tête à tête* in *Universal News Service* 7/25/1925; see also *Denver Post* 7/26/1925, *News-Palladium* 7/30 and 8/1, 5/1925; *Evening News* 7/31/1925. Ed Hughes remembers Dempsey-Greb in *Brooklyn Daily Eagle* 2/26/1933. Kearns to Menke 7/6/1919, Kearns to Runyon *(Universal Service)* 4/27/1931; Kearns reportedly said "I ducked Greb" in 1928 and added, "And if he hadn't ditched me I'd have ducked Tunney"; see *Boston Globe* 6/5/1928. Westbrook Pegler claimed that Dempsey admitted that "in a fight of the conventional 10 rounds when he and Greb were at their best Greb probably would have won the title" (11/16/1937). Interestingly, Greb is never mentioned in the legendary champion's autobiography: *Dempsey* (1977 © Jack Dempsey and Barbara Piatelli Dempsey).

V. Night and Day
The Silent Martin bout and injury in *St. Louis Post-Dispatch* 9/17, 19, 20/1919; *Akron Beacon Journal* 10/3/1916, *Press and Sun-Bulletin* (Binghamton, NY), *Wilkes-Barre Times-Leader* 10/1/1919, 4/2/1920. Boils "a problem for local boxers" in *Pittsburgh Gazette-Times* 12/23/1919; *St. Louis Star and Times* 9/19/1919, *Patriot* 9/27/1919, *Pittsburgh Daily Post* 9/29/1919. Removed cast in *Pittsburgh Press* 10/23/1919; another injury in *Repository* 10/16/1919, *Gazette-Times* 10/16, 26/1919. Dorothy's birth in *Daily Post* 10/17, 30/1919; *Repository* 10/17/1919, *Gazette-Times* 10/17/1919; Dorothy Greb's Parish/Sacramental records courtesy of Dennis Wodzinski and Suzanne Johnson of the Diocese of

Pittsburgh's Archives and Records Center. To Cleveland: *Repository* 11/14/1919 and *Tulsa World* 11/19/1919. Thanksgiving bout in *Pittsburgh Press* 11/18/1919. Soldier Jones in *Buffalo Enquirer* 11/29/1919. Panama Joe Gans incident reconstructed using the following reports: *Syracuse Herald* (12/1, 2, 3/1919) *Post-Standard* (Syracuse; 12/1, 2, 3/1919), *Syracuse Journal* (12/1, 2, 3/1919). Context provided by U.S. Census Reports 1900 and 1910; *Wilmerding News* 9/2/1904. In the district of Turtle Creek, PA where the Reillys had moved by 1910, I found no more than two black couples in the area. *American Catholic: The Saints and Sinners Who Built America's Most Powerful Church* (© 1997 Chester R. Morris) was also useful for context. [*Note:* In Boston, where, Jennifer Wohlfarth told me Mildred's parents originally settled before relocating to Pennsylvania, Irish-American antipathy could get dramatic. In February 1919, Battling Levinsky was given the referee's decision over the "Dublin Giant" Jim Coffey at Mechanic's Hall. A Jewish fan of the Jewish winner let his enthusiasm get the better of him and hollered: "Three cheers for Levinsky!" At last look, said one report, he was "still ten jumps ahead of a crowd of wild-eyed Irishmen as they raced across Boston Commons." *Buffalo Commercial* 2/13/1919.] Willie Langford bout in *Buffalo Enquirer* 3/12, 19/1918; UP 3/19/1918, *Buffalo Courier* 3/17, 19/1919; *Buffalo Commercial* 3/15, 16/1919. George Robinson in *Boston Globe* 5/19/1919, *Boston Herald* 8/25/1919, *Bridgeport Evening Farmer* 8/26/1919, *Gazette-Times* 8/27/1919.

See also *Pittsburgh Courier* 3/13/1926. Photograph of promotional flyer in *Live Fast, Die Young: The Life and Times of Harry Greb* (© 2006 Stephen L. Compton). [*Note:* Norfolk is widely considered responsible for blinding Greb in his right eye in 1921. Greb's vision was 20/20 in both eyes, according to a medical exam given by military personnel on 5/7/1918.] Red Mason letter about Dempsey in *Pittsburgh Sun* 9/19/1924; Greb's question to Dempsey in *New York Times* 8/27/1926. Injury to left hand in *Daily Post* 12/11/1919. Last bout of year, broken radius and alibi in *Wilkes-Barre Times-Leader* 12/23/1919, *Pittsburgh Press* 12/29/1919, *Philadelphia Inquirer* 12/30/1919, *Daily Post* 12/20/1919, *Kalamazoo Gazette* 12/30/1919, *Gazette-Times* 1/18, 2/8/1920. "That Harry Greb intends to break all records for the number of fights every fought by any of the past or present day boxers is again shown by his manager, James Mason…" in *Daily Post* 7/11/1919.

Epilogue: The Damned and the Beautiful
Pittsburgh Press and *Gazette-Times* interviews of Father O'Connell in 1/28/1957 and 2/10/1957 editions respectively. Lyceum's location directly across the street from Epiphany Church in *Gazette-Times* 6/2/1956. Greb receives building permit for foundation for duplex and duplex itself at 253 Gross Street in *Daily Post* 7/13, 25/1924; Greb to build house on Jackson Street in *Daily Post* 4/26/1921. Mildred at Saranac Lake in *Daily Post* 4/14/1921 and *NY Daily*

New 2/12/1923. There's little question that she took up residence at Dr. Trudeau's sanitarium. Greb's mention of moving into a cottage to be close to her also points to where she was. Greb understandably kept the details of her illness quiet. Advertisement for "middle-aged woman to do housework" in *Pittsburgh Press* 1/23 and 3/24, 26/1922. Tunney "frame-up" concerns in *Minneapolis Star* 2/22/1923, *United News* 2/23 and 3/20/1923, *Daily Post* 2/23/1923. Mildred's death in *Pittsburgh Press, Daily Post, Chicago Tribune, AP* 3/19/1923, Commonwealth of Pennsylvania Department of Health and Vital Statistics Certificate of Death, filed 3/19/1923; obituary in *Daily Post* 3/19/1923. Conversation with Jennifer Wohlfarth occurred on 6/29/2018. Greb's "comeback" fight in *Uniontown Morning Herald* 6/18, *Uniontown Evening Standard* 6/5/1923. U.S. Census 1900, 1910. Greb's Lincoln five-passenger coupe in *Gazette-Times* 12/9/1923. Greb's comment that Jeff Smith was "a troublesome customer" in a Lank Leonard column, 1931. Talk of marriage seven months after Mildred's death in *Daily Post* 12/8/1923. Paul Gallico recalls Greb in night club in *Daily News* 7/31/1931. It has been well-established that Greb did not dissipate nearly as much as the press portrayed and those closest to him pretty consistently state that while he enjoyed being around people and did frequent night clubs, he was usually a quiet spectator consuming a drink or two. His taking up residence at the Motor Square Hotel says much about his state of mind, however. Raids and other troubles at the hotel in *Daily Post* 11/9/1923, 2/17, 2/20/1925; *Gazette-Times* 4/20/1924, and *Pittsburgh Press* 1/21, 2/20/1925. Greb's trouble sleeping without a light on in *The Plain Speaker* (Hazleton, PA) 8/12/1946. Louis Walton fiasco: U.S. Census 1920, *Chicago Tribune* 12/19/1924, *Gazette-Times* 12/20/1924, 1/1, 5, 6, 9/1925; *The Montreal Gazette* 12/22/1924, *Boston Globe* 12/24/1924, 1/5/1925, *Mount Carmel Item* 1/5/1925, *Harrisburg Evening News* 1/5/1925, *Philadelphia Inquirer* 1/6/1925, *The Bee* 8/29/1925. Dice game covered in *Gazette-Times* 3/6/1925, *Daily Post* 3/12/1925; incidents at Highland Park in *Gazette-Times* 3/2/1925, *Daily Post* 3/2/1925, *Pittsburgh Press* 3/9/1925 and *Pittsburgh Press* 6/3, 6/1925; *Wilkes-Barre Evening News* 6/3/1925, *Morning News* (Wilmington Delaware) 6/4/1925, *Los Angeles Times* 6/4/1925. Greb breaking ground against Flowers and crying in the ring in *Daily Post* 2/27/1926; see also *Brooklyn Daily Eagle* 2/27/1926. Sally Bronis fiasco: *Gazette-Times* 5/5 and 8/21, 10/23/1926; *Daily Post* 5/5, 6/1926; *NY Daily News* 10/16/1926. Flowers II: *Daily Post* 8/21/1926. Greb's black patch over right eye mentioned by Damon Runyon for United Service 9/23/1926 [*Note:* Runyon also revealed, in passing, that "Greb had not been able to see out of that eye for several years."]; *Gazette-Times* 10/23/1926. "Spiritless" and death premonition in *Gazette-Times* 10/27/1926, *AP* 10/27, 28/1926 (J. Elmer Edwards quoted), and in *Gazette-Times* 10/23/1926. A world-renowned Austrian ophthalmologist, Gustav Guist, removed

Greb's eye—he grafted sheep tendons to the severed sinews inside his socket and attached a special stone eye (see *NY Daily News* 10/27/1926). Jack White's recollection of the fateful car accident in *Pittsburgh Press* 6/10/1947 and *Gazette-Times* 4/6/1948—he said the accident happened near Chester, West Virginia though later said they were driving back from Hookstown, Pennsylvania, so the best bet is that the accident occurred near the border of WV and PA. Tunney's visit to Pittsburgh in *Daily Post* 10/21/1926; Greb leaves Pittsburgh before Tunney arrives in *Gazette-Times* 10/23/1926. "Greb made every attempt to conceal the fact that he had been hurt in the smashup of his car and only his intimate friends knew that he was suffering," see *Gazette-Times* 10/23/1926 for that and other details. Complaints of severe headaches reported in *Daily Post* 10/24/1926. "Early Death of Greb Inevitable, Doctor Says" in *Gazette-Times* 10/23/1926. The "beautiful woman" at this bedside when he died was Naomi Braden. On 10/25 the AP reported that the fighter's body "will repose in a plot adjoining that in which Greb's wife...lies buried." Mildred's body was, according to *Gazette-Times* 10/26/1926, "lifted from its grave in Calvary Cemetery and placed in a new plot, where it will lie next to that of Greb's" as per his wish. Records at Calvary Cemetery state that Mildred was originally buried on 3/21/1923 in a lot in nearby section O, which was owned by Red Mason, but Dorothy Greb (Harry's sister) authorized the exhumation, transport, and reburial of her remains beside Greb in section W on 10/26/1926, which was the day before Greb's burial. Mildred left the light on.

Special thanks to my editor Deborah Green, Jennifer Wohlfarth, Alister Ottesen, Linda Asbury at Calvary Cemetery in Pittsburgh, reference librarian Lisa Robinson at the Ohio County Public Library, the staff at the Carnegie Library of Pittsburgh's Pennsylvania Department, Director Dennis Wodzinski of the Diocese of Pittsburgh's Archives and Records Center, Jose Corpas, Dino da Vinci, and Julie Cockerham.

Harry Greb's resurgence over the last ten years or so sprang primarily from the work of S.L. Compton, author of *Live Fast, Die Young: The Life and Times of Harry Greb* (© 2006 Stephen L. Compton) and Bill Paxton, author of *The Fearless Harry Greb: Biography of a Tragic Hero of Boxing* (© 2009 Bill Paxton). Compton was also gracious in lending me his eyes for some fact checking and Paxton generously shared his leads and photographs. Douglas Cavanaugh is always helpful; his contributions through Facebook's "Pittsburgh Boxing: A Pictorial History" ensure that Harry Greb lives on in the 21st century.

Where have you gone Joe Rein? Most of those he mentored he never met in person, but Rein (1936-2013) bridged generations and had a hand in building legions of fighters and writers—including this one. His kindness, knowledge, and charisma have made him immortal.

When legendary Pittsburgh sports columnist and editor Roy McHugh was born, Greb was twenty-one and only thirty-nine fights into his career. McHugh wouldn't throw in the towel until the one-hundredth anniversary of Greb's whirlwind campaign of 1919. He died not ten miles from the house on Gross Street where Greb carried Mildred over the threshold.

ROY MCHUGH
June 12, 1915 — February 25, 2019

About the Author

Springs Toledo is a widely-acclaimed essayist and author from Boston, Massachusetts. His work has been honored dozens of times by the BWAA since 2010 and has been featured on NPR's *Here & Now*. He is a member of the Ring 4 Veteran Boxers' Association and is a founding member of the *Transnational Boxing Rankings Board*, an all-volunteer initiative to help reform a sport gone mad.

www.SpringsToledo.com

Manufactured by Amazon.ca
Bolton, ON

17217972R00099